RULED BY RECLUSES?

Privacy, journalism and the media after the Human Rights Act

Edited by Damian Tambini
and Clare Heyward

30-32 Southampton St, London WC2E 7RA
Tel: 020 7470 6100 Fax: 020 7470 6111
info@ippr.org.uk
www.ippr.org
Registered charity 800065

The Institute for Public Policy Research (ippr), established in 1988, is Britain's leading independent think tank on the centre left. The values that drive our work include delivering social justice, deepening democracy, increasing environmental sustainability and enhancing human rights. Through our well-researched and clearly-argued policy analysis, our publications, our media events, our strong networks in government, academia and the corporate and voluntary sector, we play a vital role in maintaining the momentum of progressive thought.

ippr's aim is to bridge the political divide between the social democratic liberal traditions, the intellectual divide between the academics and the policy makers and the cultural divide between the policy-making establishment and the citizen. As an independent institute, we have the freedom to determine our research agenda. ippr has charitable status and is funded by a mixture of corporate, charitable, trade union and individual donations.

Research is ongoing, and new projects being developed, in a wide range of policy areas including sustainability, health and social care, social policy, citizenship and governance, education, economics, democracy and community, media and digital society and public private partnerships. We will shortly embark on major new projects in the fields of social justice, overseas development and democratic renewal.

For further information you can contact ippr's external affairs department on info@ippr.org.uk, you can view our website at www.ippr.org and you can buy our books from Central Books on 0845 458 9911 or email ippr@centralbooks.com.

Production & design by **EMPHASIS**
ISBN 1 86030 186 X

Contents

Preface

The behaviour and regulation of the press has again come under scrutiny, and is being widely debated in a manner not seen since the death of Diana, Princess of Wales.

The regulation of broadcasting standards is about to undergo the most far-reaching shake-up for a generation (as the new regulator OFCOM develops a privacy code for electronic media). And the Human Rights Act has, it is argued, introduced new forms of legal redress for those who feel their privacy has been invaded by journalists. Those who can afford lengthy court battles are using the Human Rights Act to sue newspapers that print material obtained through intrusive means, bypassing the Press Complaints Commission (PCC), the industry-funded regulatory body. The PCC has frequently been criticised for being too soft on the press, especially the tabloids. The departure of its influential Chairman, Lord Wakeham, has prompted many calls for reform of the PCC and a rethink about how a person's privacy can be protected, and the regulation of the media.

This publication from the Institute for Public Policy Research (IPPR) is a collection of papers by experts in media policy and law. It makes recommendations for new regulatory frameworks which effectively protect an individual's right to privacy, whilst paying sufficient regard to the importance of free and independent media in a democratic country.

Acknowledgements

This IPPR publication was made possible by the generous support of the BBC, Bloomberg, the Broadcasting Standards Commission, Discovery Networks Europe, the Gulbenkian Foundation, the Independent Television Commission, ITV Networks, OFTEL, the Oxford University Programme in Comparative Media Law and Policy, PACT and Turner Broadcasting.

We extend particular thanks to the Broadcasting Standards Commission for their additional input, in collaborating over the organisation of the seminar *In the Public Interest? Privacy and Media Intrusion since the Human Rights Act*, on 23 January 2002, at which early versions of all these papers were presented.

Many people helped make this publication possible. We would like to thank all those who took part in the seminar for the comments given on the papers. In particular we would like to thank Andrea Millwood-Hargreave and Donia Moinan at the Broadcasting Standards Commission, Helen Mountfield of Matrix Chambers and Clive Soley MP for their helpful contributions. We would also like to thank staff and interns at IPPR, especially Matthew Taylor, Jamie Cowling, Helena Scott, Juliane Wesemann, and Hann Ho. The views expressed, however, remain the responsibility of the authors.

About the authors

Professor Eric Barendt has been Goodman Professor of Media Law at University College London since 1990. He was previously Fellow and Tutor in Law, St Catherine's College, Oxford 1971-90. He is the author of many books on aspects of media law: *Freedom of Speech* (1987), *Broadcasting Law* (1995) and *Libel and the Media* (1995), all published by Oxford University Press

Lord Alf Dubs was a member of the Broadcasting Standards Council between 1988 and 1994, and became Deputy Chairman in 1995; he also served as Deputy Chairman of the Broadcasting Standards Commission until 1997. Lord Dubs was, from 1997 until December 1999, Parliamentary Under-secretary of State, Northern Ireland Office. He has been Deputy Chairman of the Independent Television Commission since July 2000. Lord Dubs has spent much of his career in politics, both at local and national level. He was Member of Parliament for Battersea between 1979 and 1987.

Clare Heyward has worked on various projects for the IPPR Media Programme since 2000, on both freelance and full-time bases. As well as media policy, her research interests include education policy and human rights. She is also co-author of *Curriculum Online* (IPPR 2001).

Professor David Morrison is currently Professor of Communications Research at the University of Leeds. He has held research posts at the University of Leicester, the City University and the now-defunct Broadcasting Research Unit. He has also worked in market research as a Director, and Head of Media, at Research International.

Called to the Bar in 1989, **Rabinder Singh QC** specialises in public law, human rights law and employment law. He is a member of the Panel of Junior Counsel to the Crown and is additional Junior Counsel to the Inland Revenue (common law). He appears regularly for and against public bodies. He is a Visiting Fellow at Queen Mary, London and author of *The Future of Human Rights in the United Kingdom* (published by Hart, 1997).

James Strachan is a barrister at 4-5 Gray's Inn Square.

Michael Svennevig is Director of the Research Centre for Future Communications at the University of Leeds. The Centre was established in 1976 to chart social and technological change in the UK and to act as a forum to bring academic and industry research strands closer together. He has also worked in the Broadcasting Research Department of the BBC, in the Research Department of the former IBA and at senior level in commercial media research organisations.

Damian Tambini joined IPPR in February 1999 as Senior Research Fellow. He is head of the Programme for Comparative Media Law and Policy at Oxford University. His research interests include media and telecommunications policy and democratic communication. His books and collaborations include *Cyberdemocracy* (Routledge 1998) *Markets, Citizens and States* (Oxford University Press 2001), *Communications, Revolution and Reform* (IPPR 2001) *Nationalism in Italian Politics* (Routledge 2001) and *Collective Identities in Action: Understanding Ethnic Conflict* (Ashgate 2002).

Lord John Wakeham was Chairman of the Press Complaints Commission from January 1995 until January 2002. He is a chartered accountant. Before entering politics had a large accountancy practice and was at one time on 62 company boards. His special interests are finance, business and taxation, energy, agriculture, and European matters.

Summary of IPPR recommendations

The introduction of the Human Rights Act has allowed some individuals who are the subject of unwanted media attention to defend their claims to privacy in the courts. This has led to debate about whether the courts or the current regulators are best placed to protect individual privacy, and widespread confusion about the role of the current regulatory bodies, especially the system of press self-regulation.

We argue that:

- unless the role of the regulators and courts is clarified, a two-tier regulatory system will emerge where those who can afford legal action will either challenge the regulators' decisions in the courts, or bypass the regulators entirely.

Such a system would be to the detriment of privacy protection because:

- it would provide different levels of privacy protection based on ability to meet the high costs of legal action.
- the 'double jeopardy' faced by media who are the subject of privacy claims entails significant regulatory overlap, leading to confusion and waste of resources.
- court rulings on cases brought by those rich enough to instigate legal proceedings will mean that privacy law is developed in a way that looks after the interests of a tiny proportion of the population.

IPPR recommends that:

- press self-regulation should continue but requires urgent reform.
- a full and free debate about the future of self-regulation of the press must be allowed to take place. Without a new debate, the problems outlined above will never be solved, which would be to every stakeholder's disadvantage.
- part of that debate should focus on clarifying the tired and ambiguous idea of 'the public interest'. In particular, it must be made clear that the fact that a large proportion of the population have a superficial interest in a story does not alone constitute sufficient reason for publishing a story.

- journalists must reaffirm their commitment to providing quality news of genuine importance and undertake to intrude into personal privacy only for matters that will have an impact on people's lives.
- newspapers should appoint a readers' ombudsman to deal with complaints. The ombudsman must be independent from the editor.

The current broadcast and press regulators should:

- affirm the principles of the Human Rights Act and modify their codes to comply with its provisions, and to cover new surveillance technologies.
- affirm their commitment to protecting privacy, perhaps by introducing tougher sanctions against media who intrude on an individual's privacy for no good reason.
- reform or design new procedures where necessary to ensure that their actions are transparent and publicly accountable. Negotiation behind closed doors increases public scepticism.
- ensure an adequate balance between lay people and experts on adjudication panels. Both are needed if a regulator is to keep in touch with the public mood and remain sensitive to media issues.

Government should:

- monitor case law and regulatory adjudication on media privacy and appoint an independent panel to review it in 2004.
- announce immediately that it may have to introduce a privacy law during the next Parliament to clarify privacy rights should the HRA continue to create confusion.

1. Introduction

Damian Tambini and Clare Heyward

Journalists are afforded a licence to pry which extends far beyond that enjoyed by ordinary citizens or most private companies. Hidden microphones, long lens photography and stings are the most notorious tools of investigatory journalism. These methods – and journalistic freedom in general – should be robustly defended by anyone who believes in democratic government. Where there is a strong public interest in investigation by journalists, then all should agree that privacy rights can be waived.

But who should decide when those rights should be waived, particularly in a situation in which information and images gained through intrusive means can have huge financial worth? The delicate issue of regulation of press and broadcast journalism continues to generate intense debate, because there continues to be a strong incentive for journalists to push boundaries and bend rules under an all-inclusive banner of press freedom.

Since the coming into force of the 1998 Human Rights Act, many argue that the regulation of journalists is undergoing a fundamental shift that could require further regulatory reform, or even new legislation to ensure that the optimal balance of journalistic freedom and responsibility can be attained. In this introduction, we set out the legal changes and context that are currently creating policy uncertainty and debate.

Why do journalism and privacy matter?

The media are essential to democracy. Journalists through the broadcast and print media play a vital role in keeping the public informed about the workings of government, Parliament, the economy, public authorities and international politics. The press and broadcasters can expose corruption, hypocrisy and waste. But they are also involved in a business in which intimate private facts can be sold for six-figure sums. That is why law and regulation has in the past struggled to balance freedom with responsibility.

Where journalists abuse their legitimate role and rights, the result is genuine harm not only to the immediate victims, but to the very ideals of journalistic privilege and freedom. The cost to individuals is clear. The more insidious harm is where the power to intrude impacts on society as a whole. At times we look to journalists to 'name and shame', but if that power is held arbitrarily or for illegitimate uses, the result could be a reluctance to put one's head above the parapet or speak out in public. However, if journalists are reluctant to expose wrong-doing, then clearly society will suffer.

There is a broad consensus that privacy is an inherent value worthy of protection. There are certain aspects of our lives that we go to great lengths to protect from public view. Some of these relate to our personal lives, our bodies, our intimate actions and our thoughts. Where we feel that others enter this private realm uninvited, the sense of personal harm can be great and where we think that this private realm is under threat of invasion, the scope of personal freedom or autonomy is reduced. But privacy must be balanced by the public's right to know. We accept that there are some things society has a right to know about. There are some general and defensible reasons for which we might need some access to some people's private lives. These might apply to all kinds of people, not just 'public figures', where democracy relies on a watchdog role for the media, and journalists might defend intrusions of privacy in terms of a broader public interest.

Admitting that there are some cases in which a public interest defence can justify invasion of privacy by journalists places the journalistic profession in a quasi-juridical role with unclear responsibilities. There is no warrant issued for a journalistic investigation or surveillance operation, whether that is an investigation of you, me or Prince Harry. Editors of newspapers observe the code of the PCC and broadcasters their own codes of practice and the BSC and ITC codes. The National Union of Journalists (NUJ) also has a code of practice which regulates the conduct of its members.[2]

This is not a new policy issue. Striking the necessary balance between freedom of expression and the right to privacy has been the subject of continual debate. The dangers of tipping the balance too far in favour of privacy protection are clear: over-demanding codes of practice and common law or statutory restrictions which impede journalistic investigation. On the other hand, ineffective protection leads to abuse as journalists push the boundaries of proper investigation and experiment with new technologies of surveillance. And behind public nervousness about this area is a sense that information gained in an intrusive way could be used to put pressure on public figures even when there is no broader public interest in publication. Where private lives are fair game, there is evidence that this has an adverse effect on the willingness of individuals to enter public life. The indiscriminate nature of intrusion might for example explain the difficulty of getting good candidates to stand for Parliament.

The need for a new balance

The main catalyst for change has been the passing of the Human Rights Act in 1998 (HRA), which came into force in October 2000. The Act enshrined the European Convention on Human Rights into UK law, which includes both the right to privacy (Article 8) and the right to freedom of expression (Article 10).

Article 8 and Article 10 of the ECHR

Article 8 – Right to respect for private and family life

1. Everyone has the right to respect for his private and family life, his home and his correspondence.
2. There shall be no interference by a public authority with the exercise of this right except such as is in accordance with the law and is necessary in a democratic society in the interests of national security, public safety or the economic well-being of the country, for the prevention of disorder or crime, for the protection of health or morals, or for the protection of the rights and freedoms of others.

Article 10 – Freedom of expression

1. Everyone has the right to freedom of expression. This right shall include freedom to hold opinions and to receive and impart information and ideas without interference by public authority and regardless of frontiers. This article shall not prevent States from requiring the licensing of broadcasting, television or cinema enterprises.
2. The exercise of these freedoms, since it carries with it duties and responsibilities, may be subject to such formalities, conditions, restrictions or penalties as are prescribed by law and are necessary in a democratic society, in the interests of national security, territorial integrity or public safety, for the prevention of disorder or crime, for the protection of health or morals, for the protection of the reputation or rights of others, for preventing the disclosure of information received in confidence, or for maintaining the authority and impartiality of the judiciary.

The introduction of the HRA has encouraged a new wave of challenges to the media on privacy issues in the UK courts. There has been a series of high profile court cases involving privacy claims. The HRA has already been used to challenge or bypass the authority of the current regulatory bodies.

The HRA is not, however, the only reason to reopen the debate about privacy and journalism. Current regulatory, market, technological and social changes must also be considered:

Regulatory changes

- The creation of the new communications regulator, OFCOM, as detailed in the 2002 Communications Bill and the previous White Paper (DTI/DCMS 2000).

  OFCOM will assume all content and licensing functions of the five main communications regulators: the ITC, the BSC, OFTEL, the Radio Authority and the Radiocommunications Agency. OFCOM will have to regulate in a converging environment and will preside over the transition to digital and a likely fragmentation and diversification of TV services.

Market developments

- The shift to a more economically competitive media market

  Broadcasting, in particular is becoming more competitive across channels, and the Government is committed to encouraging market entry and competition. In news this is likely to increase pressure for the premium stories that drive take-up. There are a number of likely developments that could impact on how the media treat individuals' privacy. It is feared that increased competition for viewers might lead to a general reduction in standards.

- Changes in the profession of journalism

  An increasing number of journalists are now freelancers who face an increasing pressure to 'prise up the pavement' for publishable stories. Professional regulation through the NUJ and journalism schools will get even weaker.

Technological changes

- Surveillance that is more accessible, widely available and harder to detect

  'Fresh advances in technology had to enlarge the scope for intrusion' (Neill 1999). The near ubiquity of CCTV is likely to make cases like that of Geoff Peck, in which a CCTV captured a suicide attempt, more frequent.

- The growth of internet publication

  Internet publication models present new questions concerning when material can be considered published, the degree of harm associated with publication, and the jurisdiction of self-regulatory organisations for press websites (Neill 1999).

Social changes

- A more pluralistic society

  We all recognise the need for some boundaries between public and private but we no longer live in a society with one moral code defining the boundary. Some people are happy being open about their lifestyles, others are not. The lack of a common definition creates difficulties for journalists and for those adjudicating on breach of privacy.

- Growth of the celebrity cult

  People are eager to consume stories about celebrities' lives, and also to gain fame by throwing their lives open to all. From talk shows to the 'reality TV', many people actively seek media attention, public glory or even ridicule. In many occupations, professional success entails a degree of publicity. Some may, however, still wish to keep some aspects of their lives to themselves. A person may find themselves overtaken by events and involved in a news story. Some may later try and turn this to their financial advantage and invite media attention by selling their side of the story. The main challenge posed is what to do when anyone, politician or film star, who has courted publicity in the past wishes to keep back some aspects of his or her private life. Have they forfeited privacy rights?

These changes prompt a number of questions which form the subject matter of this book:

- What has been the impact of the Human Rights Act?
- What is the appropriate relationship between existing codes of practice, self-regulatory authorities and the Human Rights Act?
- How can we avoid a damaging and wasteful process of double jeopardy and the lack of clarity and certainty that will ensue?
- How can we create a system where effective privacy protection is available to all, regardless of resources?
- Can self-regulation be reformed to create a credible alternative to legal action?
- What framework should there be for OFCOM and is there a need for a framework for the internet?
- How should regulation of journalistic intrusion be organised? What is the role of the courts versus statutory or self-regulation?

Privacy and journalism: the background

Warren and Brandeis (1890) outlined the classic statement of privacy rights, derived from common law decisions in the UK and elsewhere as 'the right to be left alone'. Until recently, few would have claimed that UK citizens enjoy a 'right to privacy'. In media and press regulation in the UK, a sectoral and self-regulatory approach has developed, with statutory codes for broadcasting and the self-regulation of the press. Many would argue that the incorporation of the European Convention on Human Rights into UK law establishes a right to privacy, with far-reaching implications for privacy and the media.

Do we need a right to privacy?

Although privacy was only recently recognised in English law, there exist a number of laws concerning the limits of freedom of expression and the conduct of journalists. Many of these have acted as imperfect proxies for privacy laws. Laws relating to harassment, breach of confidence, libel, malicious falsehood, nuisance, trespass or defamation have all been used in cases where privacy has been invaded[3]. For example, when the *Sunday Sport* sneaked into Gordon Kaye's hospital ward and published pictures and a report including quotes from the actor, his lawyers won damages by citing laws of malicious falsehood. The judge accepted that the newspaper had been wrong to say it had obtained an interview with Mr Kaye because he was in no state to give proper consent (*Kaye v Robertson* [1991]). Libel and defamation laws have similarly been stretched into use in cases involving journalistic intrusion. Conceptually however, libel and privacy cannot be reduced to one another. Since the Human Rights Act, a newspaper might successfully defend a libel case by proving the facts it reported are true but fall foul of a privacy suit, which is more concerned with whether the report should have been published at all, regardless of accuracy.

Harrassment and privacy are certainly related, many of the complaints about media intrusion centre on the complainant feeling 'hounded' by the media, 'door-stepped', or pursued down the street by dozens of journalists and cameras. NUJ, PCC and BSC codes on harassment are make it fairly clear that these sorts of practices are unacceptable and journalists also face the additional deterrent of the general law on harassment. However invasions into privacy do not have to involve harassment – reading or publication of someone's diary would constitute an invasion into privacy, even if the diary had simply been found on the street – and although privacy is mentioned in self-regulatory codes, few until recently have claimed that there is additional statutory protection.

Laws concerning breach of confidence are perhaps the closest to a privacy law in the UK and it is expected that judges might set precedents relating to privacy by developing and extending the laws of confidence (see Chapter 4). However, the two concepts are far from interchangeable. Laws of confidence are primarily concerned with transmission of information between persons who have some sort of relationship, familiar, professional or otherwise. When there is no prior relationship between the two parties, there can be no breach of confidence. By contrast, privacy can be upheld against strangers, even institutions. The information aspect of confidence also sets it apart from privacy. A sexual relationship is certainly private but it is debatable as to whether information is passed from one party to another.

A consensus among legal experts has supported the view, therefore, that the harms done in intrusions into privacy are not adequately captured by the alternative laws, and this has led many to support the introduction of a more general right of privacy. In discussing the HRA, the then Lord Chancellor stated that it was likely to lead to the emergence of a common law right to privacy (cited in Tomlinson, 2002). The events since that speech, however, demonstrate that the path to a right to privacy is far from smooth.

How privacy has been protected

Although there have been no general laws there have been detailed codes of practice enforced by regulators. The most common way of protecting privacy – and the only way before the HRA – has been to complain to the relevant regulatory body, the Press Complaints Commission (PCC), a self-regulatory body, in the case of newspapers, and the Broadcasting Standards Commission (BSC), or the Independent Television Commission (ITC), both statutory bodies, in the case of television or radio programmes. Making a complaint costs no more than the price of a stamp. The BSC requests evidence from both parties and holds a series of hearings; the PCC sees its role more as a conciliator and has a more informal process. One advantage of this system is its accessibility to ordinary citizens.

Self-regulation and the threat of legislation

Self-regulation has a chequered past in the UK. Since the Royal Commission on the Press in 1949, opposed ranks of journalists and government have repeatedly squared up and retreated. Scarce secrets about the well-known sell newspapers and journalists inevitably succumb to the temptation to push the boundaries of acceptable invasion of privacy in order to gather those stories. Over time, standards slip and public offence results. The politicians respond with the threat of statutory regulation, for example, the then Heritage Secretary David Mellor's memorable warning in 1990 that the press were 'drinking in the last chance saloon'. The press cry foul and wave the banner of press freedom whilst pulling strings in the background to clean up their act and diffuse the threat of statutory regulation. The PCC was reformed following the report of the Calcutt Review. After the death of Diana, Princess of Wales, it revised its code again and introduced stricter rules on the use of paparazzi photographers. By now the rhythm of threat and self-regulatory development is familiar. As Peter Preston put it in *The Guardian*: 'Politicians want sharper teeth and penalties. Lawyers support any initiative that includes loads of lawyers and doesn't restrict a subsequent trip to the courts. And nothing is really resolved. The saloon of last chance is always open.' (Preston 2001)

Privacy since the Human Rights Act

Despite Peter Preston's somewhat jaded description of policy in this field, the legislative and policy framework has now been fundamentally altered by the coming into force of the Human Rights Act (HRA) in 2000. The HRA requires regulators and judges to strike an appropriate balance between 'freedom of speech' and the 'right to private life'.

In the case of broadcasting, the ITC reviewed its code of practice in the light of the HRA in 2000. The relevant articles of the European Convention on Human Rights have been incorporated into the ITC code. The same is not true of the BSC code.

Since the HRA came into force, several high-profile cases have been brought which relate to journalistic intrusion into the privacy of public figures. These include:

- *R on application of Anna Ford v Press Complaints Commission*
- *Douglas, Zeta-Jones, Northern Shell plc v Hello Ltd*
- *A v B and C*
- *Sara Cox v The Sunday People*

The newsreader Anna Ford unsuccessfully challenged a PCC rejection of her complaint of privacy invasion. The judges took the view that the PCC was the body best-placed to judge on privacy issues *R on the Application of Anna Ford v Press Complaints Commission*. A few months later, however, the Douglas-Zeta-Jones and *OK!* case became the first where a UK judge acknowledged the right to privacy. Although the Court of Appeal overturned an injunction against *Hello!* allowing it to print pictures of the Hollywood stars' wedding, the Court did so on the basis that the stars were likely to establish their right to privacy in a later court case.

Commentators at the time expected this to be the start of judge-made privacy law. This is far from certain however, as the case of A v B plc and C shows – a premier league footballer was first granted an injunction prohibiting publication of his extra-marital affairs. This was overturned in the Court of Appeal on the basis that one of his former lovers had the right to publicise her story (A v B and C [2002]). The Sara Cox case has yet to come to court. Ms Cox complained to the PCC after the *Sunday People* published pictures of her on her honeymoon. The *Sunday People* apologised, but Ms Cox decided to seek redress from the courts without waiting for the PCC to adjudicate, a clear indication of a lack of confidence in the PCC.

These cases have caused intense speculation and debate. Their outcomes look set to determine the way privacy, celebrity and media is handled for many years and they also signal a need for broader policy thinking in this area. Are the current legal and regulatory arrangements the best way of achieving the delicate balance between freedom of speech and the public's right to know? Given the recent legal, technological, social and market developments we need new thinking in this area. This is the focus of this book.

The need for a new debate

The debate about regulation of journalists in the UK has been for the most part a stale and repetitive one. All too often, attempts to address the situation are dismissed as 'an attack on press freedom'. This attitude must change if we are to maintain the media's freedom and understand its proper role. It goes without saying that the HRA should not be used by anyone to 'gag the media' arbitrarily. The challenge is to create rules that permit all the freedom of expression desirable in a democracy and protect individuals in and out of the public eye from being unfairly put under the microscope. The following chapters suggest ways a balance may be struck.

Eric Barendt argues the case for statutory regulation of the press. He argues that if privacy is to be seen as a fundamental human right, then it is not appropriate for a self-regulatory body to uphold it. The current self-regulatory body has no power and varying inclination to censure the press for breaches of individual privacy. Barendt suggests areas where legislation would help clarify and protect the right to privacy.

Barendt also highlights the problem of defining the 'public interest', which is frequently used as justification for invading a person's privacy. There is a certain amount of confusion with this concept, with some editors seemingly thinking it means 'relevant to public (political) life' and others thinking it means 'matters of great interest to the public'. These two definitions can overlap, but they are by no means interchangable.

Lord Wakeham, in his final public speech as Chairman of the Press Complaints Commission, takes the opposite view, and argues the case for keeping self-regulation of the press and resisting the temptation to leave privacy issues to the courts. In particular, he argues against statutory legislation, saying that a tort of privacy is not only philosophically unjustifiable in a democracy, but it is unworkable. Most people would not be able to use a privacy law, due to the high costs of bringing a case to court. Unscrupulous editors would then be able to print all manner of intrusive material, safe in the knowledge that most people would never have the opportunity to obtain redress. In defence of the PCC, he argues that the best regulatory system is one easily available and affordable to everyone. Questions are begged in his robust defence of self-regulation. His assertion for instance that 'editors think twice before breaching the code' should be seen as a weakness of the self-regulatory system. If the code has a broad definition of public interest, surely the aim would be for editors not to breach it at all?

The barristers Rabinder Singh and James Strachan give a legal analysis of the Douglas-Zeta-Jones and *OK!* against *Hello!* appeal, the case being the first under which the courts recognised a legal right to privacy. They argue that despite a long tradition of judicial deference to regulatory bodies, the courts are able to judge privacy issues when the need arises and adopt a flexible, contextualised approach, which will ensure that the balance does not tip against freedom of expression. However, it is important to ensure that the development of privacy case law must not be too heavily based on the current laws of confidentiality.

Confidentiality issues may be closely linked to privacy issues, but if the two are conflated the result will be an impoverished form of privacy protection.

Lord Dubs highlights both the strengths and limitations of one type of statutory regulation. He argues that a light touch is needed in a statutory body, and does not support the idea that the regulator should be able to censor broadcasters. He also rejects the idea that broadcasters should be fined for transgressing codes, arguing that lighter sanctions such as requiring the broadcast and publication of adjudications will suffice. He says this makes broadcasters take notice, but the lighter sanctions mean that broadcasters are more willing to co-operate with the regulator and take the criticism on board.

All authors agree that there is a category of investigations in which a degree of intrusion is justified and that the regulatory challenge is to decide whether such investigations are really in 'the public interest'. David Morrison and Michael Svennevig present research that examines what members of the public and media experts view as in the 'public interest'. They find that the majority of the public concurs on the sort of stories that should be reported in the media, and can distinguish easily between 'real news' and gossip. He argues that the concept of 'public interest' is of no use in justifying intrusions into privacy, and a new concept of 'social importance' which is more flexible and contextual is needed.

Finally, we at IPPR argue that the current system permits great inequalities in ability to live a private life and ability to gain redress. There is clearly a danger that case law will be heavily biased towards the interests of those able to exploit the HRA for commercial or other personal gain. Reforming the self-regulatory system is preferred to privacy legislation in the first instance, although if reforms fail, or are not implemented, then the Government must step in. We recommend a number of policies for both press and broadcasting regulators, including the use of a graded, contextualised approach to privacy and public interest and call for a fresh commitment from journalists and regulators to strong news values. Privacy and media intrusion has been the topic of debate for over a century. We hope that this book will contribute to some improvement in its regulation in the UK.

Endnotes

1. The full text of these codes can be found at: www.pcc.org.uk, www.itc.org.uk, www.bsc.org.uk and www.nujonline.org.uk.
2. For a survey, see Neill B 'Privacy: A Challenge for the Next Century' in *Protecting Privacy* (OUP 1999)

References

A v B and C [2002] (Jack, J) All ER 449 and (CA) EWCA Civ 337

Douglas, Zeta-Jones, Northern Shell plc v Hello! Ltd [2001] 2 WLR 992

DTI/DCMS (2000) *A New Future For Communications* Cm 5010 HMSO

The European Convention on Human Rights available at www.hri.org/docs/ECHR50.html#C.SecI

HMSO (1998) The Human Rights Act 1998 available at www.hmso.gov.uk/acts/acts1998/80042--d.htm

Kaye v Robertson [1991] FSR 62

Neill B (1999) 'Privacy: A Challenge for the Next Century' in Markensis B (ed) *Protecting Privacy* OUP

Preston P (2001) 'It's a bit of a bodge, but the PCC is the best we've got.' *The Guardian* 3 September

R on the Application of Anna Ford v Press Complaints Commission [2001] Admin 683, 31 July

Tomlinson H (ed) (2002) *Privacy and the Media: The Developing Law* Matrix Chambers Ltd

Warren and Brandeis (1890) 'The Right to Privacy' *Harvard Law Review 193*

2. Media intrusion: the case for legislation

Eric Barendt

Traditionally English law has refused to protect privacy. But recent decisions suggest that the courts are now prepared to recognise a right protecting against media intrusion into private lives. The press has greeted these rulings with howls of protest. The former Chairman of the Press Complaints Commission, Lord Wakeham, even described one judgment as an attack on press freedom. It has been argued that legal protection for privacy will inhibit the ability of the media to investigate the probity of politicians and other public figures and so damage democracy.

However, it is right for English law to recognise a legally-enforceable right to privacy against the media. The counter-arguments of the media and their supporters are exaggerated. At the same time, it would be wrong to leave matters entirely to the courts. There is a strong case for legislation to clarify the basic rules when privacy and media freedom conflict. Hitherto, neither Conservative nor Labour governments have shown any enthusiasm for intervention in this area, largely because they are fearful of press reaction, rather than because they are intellectually convinced that it would be wrong in principle.

Why privacy is important

There is an enormous philosophical and legal literature that explains why privacy is a fundamental human right. It provides space for individuals to think for themselves and to engage in creative activity, free from observation and supervision. Further, personal relationships could not develop if participants felt that every move was watched and reported. This applies most obviously, but not exclusively, to intimate, sexual relationships.

Like the right to reputation protected by defamation laws, privacy is an aspect of human dignity and autonomy. It enables individuals to exercise some degree of independence or control over their lives. Privacy, therefore, entails rights to be alone and to keep confidential personal correspondence and other documents, and to ensure that intimate activity is not filmed or reported. Moreover, almost everyone regards privacy as essential. The instinctive and correct reply to a personal question (unless posed by a partner or a close friend) is: 'Mind your own business', whether the question is put by a journalist or by an officious bystander. Privacy is not an absolute right, any more than freedom of speech and freedom of the press, but it is sufficiently important to be guaranteed by the International Covenant on Civil and Political Rights and the European Convention on Human Rights and Fundamental Freedoms (ECHR).

The history of privacy in English law

It is surprising that English law has hitherto not recognised a right to privacy, particularly as it has historically given strong protection to the right to reputation. One explanation is that it has only been over the last hundred years that the need has arisen. There were few threats to privacy in a predominantly rural society. They emerged only towards the end of the 19th century in the wake of urbanisation, the rise of the popular national press and the development of new means for surveillance and interference with communications. But by that time the courts had become reluctant to develop the common law and establish new rights, seeing them as a matter for the prerogative of Parliament.

In 1972 the Younger Committee considered the case for establishing a general right to privacy. It rejected it, preferring to recommend the creation of remedies in specific contexts. It recommended that there should be a new tort of the disclosure or publication of information unlawfully obtained. The Law Commission has made similar proposals (see its Annual Report 1993), but Parliament has never acted on them. In 1990 a Home Office committee set up under the chairmanship of Sir David Calcutt to consider privacy protection against the press recommended against the institution of a general privacy right, at least until it was seen whether the Press Complaints Commission worked effectively to protect individuals. But it was not actually hostile in principle to the establishment of such a right.

In the last few years the courts have acknowledged that the established action to restrain breach of confidence can be used to protect privacy. This emerged, for instance, in the action brought by

Michael Douglas and Catherine Zeta-Jones against *Hello!* to stop publication of photographs in that magazine of their wedding, when the couple had given exclusive rights to publish photos to another celebrity magazine. Although two of the judges considered the claim might succeed on the basis of breach of confidence, Lord Justice Sedley preferred to regard it as a privacy action (see *Douglas, Zeta-Jones, Northern Shell plc v Hello! Ltd* [2001]). Recently, Justice Jack has granted an injunction to stop a Sunday newspaper from publishing details of the sexual relationships between a well-known (married) professional football player and two women, on the grounds that such details were confidential to the parties *A v B and C*. In essence, breach of confidence in this case, as in others, has been used to protect personal privacy.

In my view this development is long overdue, given Parliament's unwillingness to establish general legal protection for a basic human right (apart from the Data Protection Act 1998 which gives a substantial measure of protection in respect of the processing of personal data and will have some impact on the media). The Human Rights Act may have played a part in persuading the courts to act. The ECHR, incorporated in our law by the HRA, guarantees the right to respect for private life, but it is unclear whether it must be guaranteed against media intrusion as well as against interference by government and other public authorities. What is clear is that the media can argue that the enforcement of a privacy right infringes their right to freedom of expression, so in principle they should have little to fear from these legal developments.

Protection of privacy by the PCC and the BSC

Critics of privacy rights argue that the opportunity to complain to the Press Complaints Commission (PCC) offers an adequate remedy for intrusion by the print media. This system of self-regulation indeed has some merit, as does that of the Broadcasting Standards Commission (BSC) in respect of unwarranted infringements of privacy by the broadcasting media. A complaint may be made without cost and will be resolved by the PCC within a few weeks. But the existence of this procedure is not a good argument against the establishment of a legal remedy.

There are a number of reasons why it would be wrong to leave redress for privacy entirely to the PCC. Some of its weaknesses are inherent in any system of informal self-regulation. In the first place, it cannot issue any order to stop a tabloid publishing a story, even where publication clearly infringes privacy without any conceivable public interest defence. Nor can it award damages or compensation. Although editors do publish PCC rulings and journalists are required by contract to observe the Code, the print media, particularly tabloids and celebrity magazines, continue to print 'kiss and tell' stories which plainly violate the right to privacy. A legal right of action would be more likely to deter their publication. Moreover, like any law, for example, which penalises racist speech, a privacy law would set important social standards. That is why the press has been so strongly opposed to its introduction, and has been so critical of recent judgments which uphold the right at common law.

Moreover, PCC decisions in this area are far from impressive. Clause 3(ii) of the Code provides that taking photos of people in private places without consent is unacceptable. As the Anna Ford ruling shows, this provision is interpreted as implying that taking photos of people in public places is necessarily permissible (PCC 2001b). Further, the PCC held that a publicly-accessible beach was not a place where the complainants could have had a reasonable expectation of privacy, even though it was clear that they had not consented to long-range photography while they were on it wearing swimwear. Common sense suggests that people in that position have a reasonable expectation that they will be viewed only by other people on or near the beach and not by paparazzi and, through them, readers of the press. The PCC is unlikely to hold that a complainant has a reasonable expectation of privacy on a street or a car-park (PCC 2001a). In comparison, the BSC has upheld a number of complaints when film has been taken of people receiving medical attention after a traffic accident; despite being on public highways, they still had a reasonable expectation of privacy (BSC 2002a; b; c).

The PCC sometimes seems unable to distinguish between reporting which is in the public interest and reporting which the public finds interesting. How otherwise can one explain its rejections of complaints regarding the publication of the photo in hospital of the victim of a brutal attack and publication of a sequence of photographs of someone jumping to death from a bridge (PCC 1997a). The PCC is also too ready to accept the public domain argument, which can easily be used to justify infringements of privacy once a story has broken somewhere (see the William Zachs cases (PCC 1997b)).

Quite apart from these points of detail, leaving matters entirely to a system of self-regulation is wrong in principle. If privacy is a fundamental right – and clearly it is – it cannot be right to leave its protection to a body that has a significant representation from the print media (seven out of 16 members). Moreover, the Code provision is itself drafted by a committee of senior editors. Newspapers, it is said, are more inclined to take such a code seriously than they would if it were drafted by outside laymen! We would not now take this argument seriously if it were made by other enterprises. Business and trades unions are subject to general law, particularly when their activities impinge on the rights of individuals, and so should the press be.

These points do not all apply to the BSC, which is clearly independent of the broadcasting media. Moreover, its Code is more detailed and in some respects slightly more protective of privacy. In particular, the Commission is less inclined to accept the public domain argument. Clause 31 emphasises that retelling a story or examining past events may amount to an infringement of the privacy, say, of surviving victims or their relatives of a crime committed in the past, even though the material broadcast has been in the public domain. On the other hand, the Commission is unable to stop a plain breach of privacy by broadcasting journalists, say, by persistently telephoning or using hidden microphones to record a conversation, unless the programme, connected with this activity, is actually broadcast (as in *R v BCC, ex parte Barclay* [1997]). Nor can the Commission award damages or compensation, though the Broadcasting Act 1996, section 119 requires radio and television channels to broadcast a summary of the complaint and the BSC findings. Although it does not suffer the same drawbacks as press self-regulation, the BSC does not provide comprehensive privacy protection.

The case for legislative reform

The case for recognition of a legal privacy right is almost overwhelming but it does not follow that matters should be left entirely to the courts.

Judicial development of the law is slow. That means that for some time to come the law will be imprecise and uncertain. The media, particularly the tabloid press, will understandably complain that the new cause of action chills their freedom to investigate political scandal and probe the integrity of people in public life. These fears may be exaggerated but they are not groundless. It is in the interest of the media and the public for a privacy law to be as clear as it can be and provide some guidance to editors and journalists.

The best way to achieve this end is through legislation. This should set out some basic principles concerning the scope of privacy and the public interest and other defences available to the media. The application of these principles will necessarily be left to the courts and there will be room for argument in many cases, as to how the balance between privacy and freedom of the media should be struck.

Legislation could clarify the following areas:

- *The scope of privacy.* Privacy should be defined in a non-exhaustive way to cover private correspondence and papers, confidential discussions, intimate sexual conduct and health. But financial matters should be specifically excluded: the European Court of Human Rights has held that financial affairs should not be treated as an aspect of privacy (see *Fressoz & Roire v France* [2001]).

- *Publication and broadcast of photographs/images.* Some guidelines should be provided in this complex area. Publication of photographs taken without consent in a place where the complainant had a reasonable expectation that a photograph would not be taken violates privacy, subject to public interest and domain defences.

- *Public interest defence.* This defence should be expressed in non-exhaustive terms, so that the media would be able to argue that there is an overriding public interest to justify a privacy infringement in circumstances falling outside the prescribed categories. These would include: the exposure or investigation of crime, or serious misconduct, incompetence, or deception on the part of the complainant.

- *Public domain.* This defence should be available when it is clear that it can no longer be said that the material or facts for which protection is claimed still remain private. But previous publication in the media should not necessarily justify that the defence. It is not clear, for instance, that publication in a foreign newspaper or on a radio station abroad, or even temporarily on a website should inevitably mean that the information should be treated as in the public domain.

- *Remedies.* There should be some provisions about the measure of damages or compensation. In some cases exemplary or punitive damages might be appropriate, for persistent or deliberate invasion of privacy. The legislation might specify the circumstances in which it is right to proscribe publication of material which would clearly infringe privacy, although it could be arged that the HRA covers this satisfactorily.

Conclusions

It is understandable that the media, particularly the tabloid press, protest against the introduction of privacy laws. All industries – and the media industry is particularly competitive – dislike the imposition of restrictions. There is no reason to accept the argument that the development of a legal right to privacy would amount to an unacceptable and dangerous threat to press freedom. Certainly, it may deter newspapers from carrying some 'kiss and tell' stories they have hitherto been entirely free to report, exposed only to a possible smack from the PCC. But that deterrence is not necessarily wrong. Film stars, footballers and other celebrities, have rights to privacy, just as much as the ordinary citizen. We do not have a right to read about their sexual affairs or other aspects of their private life. Arguably we do not even have such a right with regard to politicians or public officials, unless there is some obvious connection between their private conduct and the discharge of their responsibilities. A politician should be as free as anyone else to say: 'Mind your own business'.

In any case, it is now much too late for newspapers to argue that privacy should not be protected at all, or that it is impossible to define satisfactorily, or that lines cannot be drawn between what should be censured and what should be regarded as legitimate matter for publication. Privacy is already a ground of complaint to the PCC which defines its scope and draws these lines. If the PCC can make these distinctions, so can the courts. The argument therefore is really not about press freedom but about the effectiveness of remedies to infringements of privacy. When the PCC itself argues against privacy laws, it cannot claim that privacy is too nebulous a concept or that the press should always be free to intrude on private life; its argument is that it is generally a better or more efficient guarantor of privacy than the courts can be. That seems an implausible argument, although there is certainly a role for an informal system of voluntary regulation to protect the interests of people who cannot afford to go to court. (But that litigation is expensive is a poor argument against legal recognition of basic human rights.)

There is some force in the contention that to leave matters entirely to the judges will mean that the law for the next few years may be uncertain. The press might conceivably overreact and refrain unnecessarily from publishing stories of genuine public interest. Therefore it would be better for the Government to have the courage to intervene and to introduce legislation to give the contours of the right to privacy more precision. On the matter of principle, we should all accept with relief that English law is at long last prepared to recognise privacy, not only when it is infringed by government but also when the media publishes personal information on matters which are none of our business.

References

The Times (2001) 'A v B and C' 10 September

HMSO (1996) Broadcasting Act, s119

Broadcasting Standards Commission (2002a) Complaints Bulletin 27 www.bsc.org.uk

Broadcasting Standards Commission (2002b) Complaints Bulletin 31 www.bsc.org.uk

Broadcasting Standards Commission (2002c) Complaints Bulletin 35 www.bsc.org.uk

Douglas, Zeta-Jones, Northern Shell plc v Hello! Ltd [2001] 2 WLR 992

Fressoz & Roire v France [2001] 31 EHRR 8

HMSO (1990) Home Office *Report of the Committee on Privacy and Related Matters* Cm1102

HMSO (1972) *Younger Committee Report on Privacy* Cm 5012 Law Commission (1993) Annual Report

Press Complaints Commission (2001a) PCC Report 53 www.pcc.org.uk

Press Complaints Commission (2001b) PCC Report 52 www.pcc.org.uk

Press Complaints Commission (1997a) PCC Report 40 www.pcc.org.uk

Press Complaints Commission (1997b) PCC Report 38 www.pcc.org.uk

R v BCC, ex parte Barclay [1997] EMLR 62

3. Press, privacy, public interest and the Human Rights Act

Lord Wakeham

Politicians come and go but some debates never change. Throughout and beyond my time in politics one question in particular has persisted: why don't we have a privacy law? And it is usually asked most vigorously by those who find what they read about themselves in the press uncomfortable.

Some principles also persist. In any debate on privacy laws, I have always had two central concerns. The first is a practical point: that privacy laws would do nothing to protect the privacy of ordinary people. They would simply be used by the rich and powerful, or the corrupt, to stop newspapers printing unpalatable truths. The second concern is a philosophical one: that a privacy law would undermine the freedom of the press which is the cornerstone of our democracy. Privacy is important, but so is free expression: the first and most vital of Roosevelt's 'four essential freedoms'.

However, not favouring a privacy law does not necessarily mean undervaluing individual privacy. Far from it. I have long seen at first hand the damage that can be wreaked by intrusive journalism and invasion of an individual's privacy. Unjustified intrusions can wreck careers and lives and should not be tolerated. The question is how we should protect that privacy. How can we ensure that genuine intrusions into personal privacy not in the public interest become fewer and further between without undermining freedom of expression? In my view, the only way is through tough and effective self-regulation by newspapers and magazines themselves.

Self-regulation: the record of the Press Complaints Commission

The protection of personal privacy is at the heart of the system of self-regulation administered by the Press Complaints Commission (PCC).

The bulk of the complaints we receive are about accuracy in reporting but it is by the handling of the 15 per cent of complaints about personal privacy that we are judged.

It is widely assumed, quite wrongly, that those alleged intrusions into personal privacy only concern national tabloid newspapers. In fact, in the year 2000 – the last year for which detailed figures have been published – only 33 per cent of privacy complaints were about national newspapers, both tabloids and broadsheets. Some 61 per cent concerned regional newspapers in England and Wales, and Scottish and Northern Irish publications. The remainder were about magazines. So privacy issues affect the entire industry from *The Sun* and *The Mirror*, to the *Birmingham Evening Mail*, the *Glasgow Evening Times*, and *Take a Break!* magazine.

Indeed, it is because the issue is relevant to all publications that the industry's Code of Practice places the protection of personal privacy at its heart. That Code sets out the benchmarks by which all editors must make judgments about possible intrusions into privacy. Echoing exactly the terms of the European Convention on Human Rights, it states that:

> Everyone is entitled to respect for his or her private life, home, health and correspondence. A publication will be expected to justify intrusions into any individual's private life without consent. (PCC Code of Practice available at www.pccc.org.uk)

Further provisions of the Code deal with more specific privacy issues including the use of photographs, the protection of children, hospitals, grief and shock and the innocent relatives and friends of people convicted of crime.

The Code also recognises that there will be times when newspapers – which play a key role in a democratic society in scrutinising those who wield influence and power – need to intrude into someone's personal life in the public interest. It therefore seeks to give some examples – which are by no means exclusive – of instances when an intrusion will be in the public interest: for instance, when a newspaper is detecting or exposing crime or serious misdemeanour; when it is protecting the public health and safety; and when it is seeking to stop the public being misled by the statement or action of an individual or organisation. It also makes clear, importantly, that there is a public interest in freedom of expression itself.

Although the system of self-regulation is far from perfect – and breaches do from time to time occur – there are two things which have to be said about the effectiveness of the Code. First, it has transformed standards in newspapers since it was established in 1991. Before then – in the 1980s when instances of irresponsible journalism led to the appointment of the Calcutt Committee – intrusions into the lives of ordinary people were all too common. Today, there are far fewer of them and where they do occur, the PCC will require a full explanation and will not hesitate to censure an editor who has breached the Code.

Secondly, editors *do* take notice of it and *do* judge potential stories against its benchmarks. This is because the Code is drafted by editors for editors. Censure of an editor by the PCC has to be published in full in his or her newspaper and is a serious professional matter: it is tantamount to saying that the editor broke his or her own rules and has therefore been censured by his or her own professional body. Editors think twice before breaching the Code and so many more stories have failed to see the light of day.

External regulation: the challenges

Could the law – either through the front door of a fully-fledged privacy tort and statutory controls, or through the back door of the Human Rights Act – do such a good job? There are three tests to apply in answering that question.

Accessibility to the general public

Firstly, any privacy law would be inaccessible to the vast majority the general public. Laws of this sort are designed only for those with money to stake on an uncertain outcome in the courts. How many ordinary people would be prepared to risk their home for such an action? How many people would be prepared to risk every detail of their private life being raked over in Court?

By contract, it is ordinary people who make use of the services of the PCC which is completely free of charge and carries out its work away from the glare of publicity and the trauma of witness box cross-examinations. Of the complaints received in 2000, some 90 per cent came from people far removed from the public eye. None of these could ever consider making use of the law but find an effective and quick form of redress through the PCC. Of all those complaints, nearly half are resolved through the PCC between the person who has suffered from some form of intrusion and the newspaper or magazine concerned. No such resolution would be available through the Court. A law might assist a few people but it could never do so on the scale or with the success of the PCC.

Minimising intrusion

That leads to my second concern about a privacy law: that it might actually make intrusions into the private lives of ordinary people more likely.

At the moment a newspaper editor knows that he or she cannot escape the demands of the Code or the scrutiny of the PCC if a mistake is made. The PCC is free, accessible and effective. But if the Code were substituted by a privacy law, a completely different situation would arise. Editors might well take the chance that someone will not be prepared to take a legal action – or be able to afford to do so – and intrude into their private lives without retribution. Any law might actually make the matter worse, not better, for ordinary people.

Resistance to misuse

My third – and perhaps most important – concern about a privacy law is the way in which some people would misuse it. Privacy laws establish a powerful arsenal for individuals who would prefer – usually for the wrong reason – that a newspaper did not scrutinise them. Injunctions would be effortlessly deployed against newspapers undertaking legitimate investigative journalism. Costly actions would deter newspapers from scrutinising the lives of the very rich or the very powerful. At a stroke, a privacy law would provide a severe blow to the ability of newspapers to investigate, scrutinise and, where necessary, intrude in the public interest. The freedom of the press would be seriously eroded.

So could a law deliver better results than self-regulation? I think not. And it is against these arguments – that a privacy law would not help those it would be intended to help, that it might actually facilitate intrusion, and that it would undermine investigative journalism – that we need to judge the implementation of the Human Rights Act 1998.

The Human Rights Act

Against this background, we need to return to the Government's initial proposals in 1997 to incorporate into UK law the European Convention of Human Rights, the purpose of which was, originally, to enlarge freedom and to curtail state power.

The Convention in context

As a document, the European Convention of Human Rights is a relatively innocuous set of principles. Much of what it contains about the right to life, the right to a fair trial and the right to freedom of expression are generally considered to be basic human rights. The key to the Convention, however, is the time that it was sculpted. In the early 1950s it was drafted by British authors as a response both to the barbarism of Nazi Germany and the Second World War and to the rise of Communism in Eastern Europe. It was welcomed by most other Western European Governments as a Convention to act as a check on state power. It was also, therefore, a set of aspirations for emerging democracies.

The 'right to privacy' contained in Article 8 of the Convention ought to be seen in that context. It was nothing to do with 'privacy' from the press but rather a protection from the intrusive power of the state, its bugging apparatus, its spying equipment, its intrusion into family life and so on. As such, it was much needed at the time.

The British Government was always a signatory to the Convention but it never enshrined it into UK law as some other continental European countries did. Britain was not yet a member of the EU and was unprepared to import alien legal concepts into its sovereign Parliamentary and judicial system. Furthermore, most of the 'rights' contained in the Convention were already taken for granted in one of the world's oldest Parliamentary democracies.

The challenges of incorporation

My fear was that the method of incorporation chosen by the Government in 1997 could have precisely the opposite effect. Indeed, so far as the free press was concerned, incorporation threatened to do precisely what the authors of the Convention sought to prevent: to undermine, rather than enlarge, freedom of expression and strengthen the power of an already powerful state at the expense of ordinary people. A document aimed at the power of the Stasi and the Gestapo could end up being used against *The Sun* or *The Guardian*.

The problem was this. As originally conceived by the Government before the 1997 General Election, the act of incorporation was to be a narrowly-based and rather technical measure that would only impinge on the actions of public authorities: Government departments, local authorities, NHS Trusts. This, in itself, seemed within the spirit of the Convention, which was after all about state power. The new, imported law was – so its proponents said at the time – never intended to apply to actions between private individuals or private enterprises.

After the election, the act of incorporation – and the method chosen – changed subtly, but with dramatic consequences. The proposal to incorporate the European Convention on Human Rights became something intended to imbue the entire legal system.

The change occurred because the method of incorporation turned the courts into public authorities with the power to 'enforce' the Convention both against government and in any private actions brought before them. This at a stroke caused wholesale erosion of Parliamentary sovereignty and gave the courts a number of new concepts with which to grapple. Chief among these was the 'right to privacy', which had been so crucial in 1950s Europe but became potentially pernicious for press freedom the United Kingdom in the 21st Century.

There had never been a right to privacy in UK law. Indeed, in the famous 1991 judgment on the Gorden Kaye case – the actor into whose hospital bedroom two photographers burst to take pictures of him while he lay critically ill – the Court ruled that the right to privacy had been so long unrecognised in UK law that it was difficult to see how the courts could begin to fashion one (*Kaye v Robertson* [1991]).

That had not meant that there was no ultimate legal redress on privacy matters. Individuals have had the option of taking an action to the Strasbourg Court and to argue, in so doing, that the British Government was not protecting their right to privacy. However, in all the actions taken against the UK Government over the last five decades – including most famously and recently by Earl Spencer – not once did the British Government lose a case because of a lack of a privacy law in this country.

The reason for that is two-fold. First the Strasbourg Court – recognising that Article 8 on privacy has to be balanced with Article 10 on freedom of expression – has always tended to give more weight to Article 10. Second, it has always ruled that there was sufficient protection for individuals both through the industry's self-regulation and in the law (through actions to protect confidence and copyright) to obviate the need for a privacy tort.

In that latter point, however, were potential problems. In its judgment on the Spencer case in early 1998, the Strasbourg Court rejected Lord Spencer's action against the British Government, arguing that he had not utilised all his potential legal protections, specifically, the law of confidence (*Spencer v United Kingdom* [1998]). Their message to the UK courts – and potential litigants – seemed to be clear: that the law of confidence could be used, if in a somewhat cumbersome fashion, to produce a backdoor privacy law, if you had the time, money and patience to use it.

That was, in effect, what the courts had already begun to do – irrespective of the Human Rights Act – and a number of cases in the mid-1990s pointed in that direction. In addition, some members of the judiciary had been agitating about the lack of a privacy law in the UK and signalled their intention to try to use the Human Rights legislation to produce one. This was despite the fact that successive governments of all political parties had declared their opposition to it. Indeed, the incoming Government in 1997 – both before and after the election – explicitly stated that it was opposed to privacy legislation on the grounds that it would compromise press freedom and that the PCC was doing an effective job.

The PCC and incorporation

The Press Complaints Commission and the newspaper industry were alive to the dangers inherent in this form of incorporation. In October 1997, I raised the issue of whether the PCC was likely to be a 'public authority' under the terms of the legislation. The consequences could have been judicial supervision of the PCC's decisions on privacy matters – including the possibility that the courts would give the PCC powers to fine as well as to exercise prior restraint – which would have undermined self-regulation altogether.

However, it soon became evident that the issue of who was or who was not a public authority was at best largely irrelevant. Because the courts were public authorities and had complete power to 'enforce' the terms of the Act, everyone would be caught up in its terms, from the local parish council to the biggest companies in the country.

Against that background, the PCC moved to see whether the Bill could be amended to protect freedom of expression. It had three principle concerns.

The first and foremost concern was the possibility that the legislation might be used by individuals and companies to obtain interlocutory injunctions against the press on grounds of privacy, something which had previously been almost impossible. The main problem was that most judges would grant such temporary injunctions to maintain the status quo while they assessed the balance that needed to be struck between Article 8 and Article 10. This would produce a significant chilling effect on a great deal of investigative journalism. As the Jonathan Aitken story, involving the *Guardian*, illustrated, most stories of corruption contain 'personal' elements where a right to privacy could be argued and were therefore at risk of prior restraint.

The second concern was about the nature of the British courts themselves. While in Strasbourg the European Court has always tended to give paramount weight to freedom of expression over rights to privacy, it was possible that British judges – some of whom had consistently made clear their desire to fashion a privacy law – might not take the same view. The concern was to find some way of importing the jurisprudence of Strasbourg into the legislation to act as a brake on any moves toward a back-door privacy law.

The third concern was the position of the PCC, the Code and self-regulation. The PCC and the industry had to find a way to signal to the courts that the Code was for the PCC to administer and also to make clear that self-regulation is in itself a clear manifestation of freedom of speech. The press has its own rights to free expression, after all: without self-regulation – independent of courts as well as of Government – the press is not free. The Government recognised these concerns and a compromise was eventually reached to amend the Bill.

Section 12: protecting freedom of expression

That amendment – on freedom of expression – eventually became Section 12 of the Human Rights Act 1998. It is not a perfect solution but it does place a number of important weapons in the arsenal of a free press and goes some way to safeguarding freedom of expression and, consequently, self-regulation. The theoretical effect of Section 12 is as follows.

First, it recognises the unique importance of the freedom of the press by outlining a special regime for journalistic, literary and artistic material. This applies not just to the Convention rights but to the development of any common law of privacy for instance on the back of alleged breaches of confidence. This is the key signal to the courts to be mindful of the Strasbourg jurisprudence and not simply to push ahead with a *de facto* privacy law on the back of Article 8.

Second, and crucially, it deals with the issue of prior restraint by setting a very high threshold at which injunctions – both under the Convention and in any development of common law – can be taken out to prevent publication. Courts will have to take account of the importance of freedom of expression, public interest, the extent to which actions were fair and reasonable and PCC Code compliance. The Act effectively reverses the burden of proof: any applicant seeking an injunction will have to prove that an article should not be published, rather than the newspaper defending its publication. This, the Government said at the time, would mean that injunctions are only likely to be granted in the most exceptional circumstances. That was, in theory at least, perhaps the most important prize of Section 12.

Third, because of its emphasis on freedom of expression, the Act improves the safeguards for articles and stories where one party to a series of events seeks to put their view forward in a newspaper, magazine or book. The Act directs courts to have regard to the extent to which material is – or is about to become – available to the public: in the age of the internet this covers a great deal of material.

Crucially, during the passage of the Bill in the House of Commons, the Home Secretary made clear that the industry's self-regulation through the Code and the PCC was something that should be 'preserved' and warned the courts not to interfere in privacy matters so long as the PCC was doing its job effectively. He said:

> The Government have always made clear our support for effective self-regulation as administered by the Press Complaints Commission under its Code of Practice. We have also said that we have no plans to introduce legislation creating a general law of privacy. On the question of prior restraint, our intention…is that the thresholds that the new clause sets will mean that interlocutory injunctions should be granted ex parte only in the most exceptional circumstances. Similarly, on self-regulation, the new clause provides an important safeguard by emphasising the right to freedom of expression. Our intention is that it should underline the consequent need to preserve self-regulation. That effect is reinforced by highlighting in the amendment the significance of any privacy code, which plainly includes the code operated by the PCC.' (Hansard 1998)

It is not a perfect amendment, by any means, but it was the best that could be achieved in the circumstances.

The Human Rights Act in practice

That, then, is the background and the theory. What has happened in practice to date and what happens from here? First and foremost, one or two myths need to be debunked.

Myths and misunderstandings

The crux of these myths – perpetrated by ill-informed commentators in the wake of the High Court's judgment in the case of Michael Douglas and Catherine Zeta Jones (*Douglas, Zeta-Jones, Northern Shell plc v Hello! Ltd* [2001]) – is that we now have a fully-fledged privacy law and that celebrities and public figures will be stampeding off to the courts and bypassing the PCC.

That picture is completely unrealistic. Firstly, the Act has been in operation since October 2000 and in the past fifteen months not one Judge or one Court has said that the Human Rights Act 'creates' a privacy law. Second, fewer than ten cases have in that time gone to Court and not one of them has produced a final ruling. That is a very small number and somewhat supports the argument that the Act has proved cumbersome, inaccessible and practically useless for ordinary people.

Third, there is absolutely no evidence that people have 'bypassed' the PCC in any way. Indeed, last year the PCC received 3,030 complaints, a record number. Of these, a record 520 related to some aspect of privacy under relevant sections of the Code.

Another myth is that there is now a two-tier system of privacy redress: the Human Rights Act for the toffs and the PCC for everyone else. In fact, in the last year the PCC has dealt with more celebrities and public figures than ever before, from JK Rowling to Cilla Black, the cast of *Emmerdale*, Vanessa Feltz, Tony Blair, the Lord Chancellor, Prince William and many other public figures, including many other well-known names, famous for different reasons, such as Primrose Shipman and Ian Brady. In every case bar two of the hundreds of privacy complaints we dealt with, the PCC – where it found a breach of the Code – has produced satisfactory redress for the individuals concerned. In only two cases have there been subsequent legal action: that of Anna Ford and of Sara Cox.

The Sara Cox case is yet to come to Court, but the issue of Anna Ford allows me to debunk another myth: that the courts are now the custodians of privacy issues. As you will know, Anna Ford complained about intrusion into her privacy. We rejected her complaint – ruling that a public beach in Majorca at the height of the holiday season was not a place where she could enjoy a reasonable expectation of privacy – and in the spring of last year she sought judicial review of that decision (only the second time in 25,000 complaints we have handled that anyone has sought to do so). In July – in a long and carefully-worded judgment – Mr Justice Silber rejected Ms Ford's application for review. Instead, he backed the PCC, and established that it was not for the courts to intervene in such matters. He made clear that:

> The type of balancing operation [between privacy and freedom of expression] conducted by a specialist body, such as the Commission, is still regarded as a field of activity to which the courts should and will defer. The Commission is a body whose membership and expertise makes it much better equipped than the courts to resolve the difficult exercise of

> balancing the conflicting rights...[of] privacy and of the newspapers to publish). (*R on the Application of Anna Ford v Press Complaints Commission* [2001])

What has given rise to so many myths? Part of it is, inevitably, propaganda spread by those with financial gain to make: there is money to be made in privacy and the Human Rights Act. But most of it is a misinterpretation of the ruling in the case of Douglas and Zeta Jones. That, many commentators said, was proof that we now had a privacy law, or at least a privacy law for the rich and famous.

In reality, the question of privacy was at best a subsidiary matter. The main issues were breach of confidence, malicious falsehood, unlawful interference with contractual relations and breach of copyright, all of which existed long before the Human Rights Act. This ruling could almost certainly have been delivered before the Human Rights legislation was on the statute book. Furthermore, what the Court did say on privacy can largely be disregarded: they had only perfunctory arguments from Counsel on the privacy points and the judges specifically said that their conclusions were very limited in this area (something the commentators completely ignored). What controversial comments were made relating to privacy were only made by one of the three Judges sitting: he was unsupported by the other two.

Even more importantly, at the heart of the ruling is this fact: that the Court refused to maintain an injunction on privacy grounds after considering the application of Section 12 of the Human Rights Act and the PCC Code. This is exactly what Section 12 of the Act was supposed to achieve and is, to some extent, an important pointer to the future. All round, this ruling is far removed from the public perception.

Genuine causes for concern

But the picture across the board is not entirely rosy. Some serious problems have emerged in two of the handful of cases that have so far arisen.

The first is the issue of the interpretation of the PCC's Code and involves the case of Mr and Mrs Attard and the *Manchester Evening News* (*MEN*). It concerns the publication of photos of Gracie Attard –

the survivor of the two conjoined twins who underwent an operation in Manchester earlier in the year – by the *MEN* on 15 June 2001.

Mr and Mrs Attard had entered into a substantial contract with two Sunday newspapers for pictures of Graci but, as a result of a good, old-fashioned scoop, the *MEN* got the pictures first and published them. In order to protect their financial interest the parents went to court to get an injunction restraining further publication and at the same time complained to the PCC under various sections of the Code of Practice.

The injunction was granted immediately restraining further use of the photos by the *MEN* or any other papers. The Order was made under the terms of the Human Rights Act 1998, specifically Section 12, which deals with freedom of expression and interlocutory injunctions. In granting the injunction – which in effect allowed the parents to protect a commercial contract under the cloak of privacy – the Court took a view about the application of the PCC's Code of Practice and how it related to this particular case. The judge concluded that the photographs were in breach of the Code. (*MGN Ltd v Attard* [2001])

As well as seeking an injunction and a legal remedy for their grievance, the Attards made a complaint to the PCC. Normally, the PCC would not be in a position to adjudicate on any matter which was the subject of legal action. But in this case, a complaint was made not just under the privacy section of the Code but under those parts relating to hospitals (Clause 9) and most importantly children (Clause 6). The PCC was therefore able to investigate and adjudicate on these complaints, although it declined to adjudicate on a complaint under the privacy Clause of the Code as this was already the subject of a Court Order.

The PCC rejected the complaints for a number of substantial reasons, including the fact that the parents had compromised their rights to their daughter's privacy and that the material concerned was about to enter the public domain. It said that:

> It is not the function of the Commission to seek to protect the financial position of complainants through the use of the privacy sections of the Code of Practice. Indeed, the Commission has always taken the common sense view that where a complainant releases or sells information or photographs then they may become disentitled to the protection of the Code in certain circumstances. Privacy is – in the

> Commission's opinion – not a commodity which can be sold on one person's terms. (Press Complaints Commission 2001)

The significance of the adjudication is that the PCC took a different approach from that of the Court which had ruled that publication was in breach of the Code. This was because the PCC was able to take into account a number of factors, including the substantial body of PCC case law on matters relating to children. Those precedents clearly relate the issue of children's privacy – and particularly that of infants – to their welfare. This is not something the Court (which could not be in possession of that information) could consider.

The central concern here is that when the Government introduced Section 12 it made clear the importance of the newspaper industry's own self-regulation, and of the PCC, rather than the courts, establishing whether the Code was breached or not. This was in view of the fact that the PCC itself is in the strongest position to do so, considering all the facts involved and taking into account important previous adjudications, as editors themselves are obliged to do.

There is great potential danger if the courts seek to place themselves in the position of the Commission, especially if they are granting injunctions on the basis of a necessarily perfunctory interpretation of the Code. It is to be hoped that this will be addressed in the Court of Appeal. The original injunction against the MEN still stands and does so as worrying precedent. It is interesting to note that in varying the injunction for the *Sunday People*, Mr Justice Connell confirmed that:

> It is apparent from the judgment of Mr Justice Bennett...that he may have misunderstood the Code of Conduct applicable to situations such as the instant situation, and in particular the Code of Conduct in so far as it refers to the publication of photographs of children. That publication is, in fact, barred where welfare is affected but there is no absolute prohibition, as the learned judge seems to have been led to understand prior to delivering that judgment.' (*MGN Ltd vs Attard* [2001])

The other case to have caused considerable concern has been well publicised and relates to a story which the *Sunday People* sought to run about a footballer who was cheating on his wife with two women. The principles involved relate to the balance between the footballer's right to privacy and the right of the two women concerned to freedom of expression.

As it stands, there seems to be great weight in the argument of those who say the injunction is an unacceptable infringement on press freedom and freedom of expression. The judgment – again made under the privacy provisions of the Human Rights Act – is drawn in such wide and stringent terms that it would make vast tracts of day-to-day journalism in the public interest quite impossible. The mischief stems from Paragraph 56 of the ruling which states that:

> In my judgment the law should afford the protection of confidentiality to facts concerning sexual relations within marriage (which is surely straightforward) and, in the context of modern sexual relations, it should be no different with relationships outside marriage. (*The Times* 2001)

There is also much merit in the arguments of those who say this is a precedent that cannot be allowed to stand. Again, it is to be hoped that when this case comes to the Court of Appeal it will be effectively dealt with.

Persistent principles and lessons to be learned

Media, and press regulation in particular, is a hugely complex and dynamic field and it might be helpful to summarise the main points.

- We all believe the right to individual privacy to be a hugely important one for every individual. It is a basic human right and intrusions into privacy can do grave damage to individuals and to families. But the right to free expression – on which every democracy is based – is equally important and an effective balance must be struck between the two.
- The main question is how to guarantee personal privacy without curtailing press freedom: through the quick and effective procedures of self-regulation or through the more cumbersome, time-consuming and costly procedures of the law. Self-regulation would seem to point the most effective way forward for the vast majority of people.

- Against that background, it was to the Government's credit that it moved to amend the Human Rights Act 1998 which had posed a grave threat to press freedom. Section 12 went a long way to protecting freedom of expression and ensuring the continued effectiveness of tough and independent self-regulation.

- Early experience shows that the Human Rights Act is of little use to ordinary people and to most celebrities, other than those who are very rich. Only very few cases have gone to Court since the Act was implemented while the number of complaints to the PCC has been increasing. That speaks volumes about the efficacy of the two systems.

- Most of those cases have yet to be decided and there is no early evidence to suggest that the courts will use the Act to fashion a privacy law. Certainly the judgment in Douglas and Zeta Jones – widely but wrongly hailed as the inauguration of a new legal regime – does not do that. The only case where there has been an actual judgment based on the Act was in Anna Ford's judicial review of the PCC in which the Court backed the Commission as the best arbiter of such disputes.

- However, there have been some very disturbing developments relating to the handing down of *ex parte* injunctions under the Act, which the Government said should be granted only in the most 'exceptional circumstances'. The Court of Appeal will have a key role to play here will take all these arguments into account. Whatever the result of individual cases, full force must be given to the proper functioning of Section 12 of the Act.

- A tough and effective system of self-regulation – available free to ordinary people and public figures alike – will continue to be the best way of maintaining press freedom and protecting the privacy of every individual, whoever they may be.

Conclusion

The issues of individual privacy, freedom of expression, self-regulation and the Human Rights Act are a complex cocktail of sometimes competing and conflicting interests. My aim as Chairman of the PCC has been to preserve self-regulation in the interests of press freedom and, more importantly, the general public.

In the coming months, there will be a number of important cases before the courts which will have some bearing on that. There are difficult decisions for the Court to make which – certainly on the issue of injunctions – will have substantial, long term ramifications for press freedom and freedom of expression.

If these decisions were to conflict with the manner in which the Press Complaints Commission operates, then a serious situation could arise, not least because Parliament itself has made clear its opposition to a privacy law and its support for the maintenance of an independent and effective system of self-regulation. However, I have every confidence that Parliament, courts, newspapers and regulators will find a just and sensible way forward to protect both the privacy of individuals and the right of free expression on which our ancient democracy stands.

References

The Times (2001) 'A v B plc & C' 10 September

Douglas, Zeta-Jones, Northern Shell plc v Hello! Ltd [2001] 2 WLR 992

Hansard (1998) 2 July 1998, col 541

Kaye v Robertson [1991] FSR 62

MGN Ltd vs Attard [2001] Family Division of the High Court of Justice, 11 October

Press Complaints Commission (2001) *PCC Report 55* October 2001 www.pcc.org.uk

R on the Application of Anna Ford v Press Complaints Commission [2001] Admin 683, 31 July 2001

Spencer v United Kingdom [1998] 25 EHHR CD105

a judical order restraining a person from an action, or compelling a person to carry out a certain act.

4. The right to privacy in English law[1]

Rabinder Singh and James Strachan

Over 110 years ago, two partners in a Boston law firm published a seminal article in the *Harvard Law Review*. Its title and its content were bold in recognising and charting that most indefinable and elusive of all rights: the right to privacy. In words as apposite today as in the US in the 19th Century, the authors were uncompromising in their identification of the importance of the right to be left alone.

> The press is overstepping in every direction the obvious bounds of propriety and decency. Gossip is no longer the resource of the idle and of the vicious, but has become a trade, which is pursued with industry as well as effrontery. To satisfy a prurient taste the details of sexual relations are spread broadcast in the columns of the daily papers. To occupy the indolent, column upon column is filled with idle gossip, which can only be provided by intrusion upon the domestic circle. The intensity and complexity of life, attendant upon advancing civilization, have rendered necessary some retreat from the world, and man, under the refining influence of culture, has become more sensitive to publicity, so that solitude and privacy have become more essential to the individual. (Warren and Brandeis 1890)

The two authors carefully analysed the development of English common law and there was a wealth of case law to support their declaration. In particular, the authors drew heavily upon the English court's decision in *Prince Albert v Strange* [1849] in which Prince Albert successfully applied for an injunction to prevent the publication of a catalogue and exhibit of private etchings. The decision heralded an important watershed in the protection afforded against breach of trust and breach of confidence and formed an important landmark for the development of these causes of action.

So Warren and Brandeis confidently declared the existence of a right to privacy protected by the law and so contributed to the development of American law. Somewhat ironically, that declaration was simultaneously followed by the almost total disappearance of recognition of the right to privacy on this side of the Atlantic. Instead, the right to privacy was first ignored and then expressly disavowed by the judiciary in England and Wales.

Kaye v Robertson: the nadir of the right to privacy

The nadir of privacy's troubled evolution is epitomised by the case of *Kaye v Robertson* [1991]. In 1990, Mr Kaye (the well-known actor of the television series *'Allo, 'Allo*) had suffered serious injuries and undergone extensive surgery to his head after a car accident. While Mr Kaye lay in hospital, journalists from the *Sunday Sport* gained access to his private hospital room, interviewed him and took pictures. In a judgment which has been subject to much criticism by commentators, the Court of Appeal expressed their powerlessness to act to protect Mr Kaye's privacy. The relief granted to Mr Kaye was limited to that which could be derived from an action for malicious (or injurious) falsehood. The newspaper was only injuncted from publishing any photographs or material which could be reasonably understood or convey to a reader that Mr Kaye had voluntarily permitted the interview.

The statements made by the Court of Appeal in Kaye concerning a right to privacy were unequivocal:

> If ever a person has a right to be let alone by strangers with no public interest to pursue, it must surely be when he lies in hospital recovering from brain surgery and in no more than partial command of his faculties. It is this invasion of his privacy which underlies the plaintiff's complaint. Yet it alone, however gross, does not entitle him to relief in English law. (*Kaye v Robertson* [1991])

Lord Justice Leggatt even went so far as to acknowledge that the recognition of a right to privacy had been in prospect as long ago as 1816 when Lord Byron had obtained an injunction to restrain the false attribution to him of a bad poem (*Byron v Johnson* [1816]). Yet Leggatt still felt unable to accept that such a right could be discerned and recast within the English common law, saying instead that:

> This right has so long been disregarded here that it can be recognised now only by the legislature.

Where American law offered protection, English law was powerless. The ability to invade privacy and to violate the right to be left alone has never been more developed and yet the right itself is in its infancy.

Unfit to judge? The recent history of privacy in judicial review

This historical reluctance of the courts to affirm the right to privacy is apparent in the recent cases where media regulators have been taken to judicial review. (In judicial review cases, the Court is naturally more deferential than in other cases.) In these cases, there have been strong statements by the courts of their unwillingness and lack of competence to deal with privacy issues. For example, in *R v Broadcasting Standards Commission ex parte British Broadcasting Corporation* [2000], Lord Woolf expounded the deference afforded to the Broadcasting Standards Commission (BSC) when applying its own code:

> So long as the approach which [the BSC] adopt is one to which, in their statutory context, the words infringement of privacy are capable of applying then the courts should not interfere. It is only if an approach to 'infringement of privacy'...goes beyond the area of tolerance that the courts can intervene. There will be situations which fall within the grey area where it will be very much a matter of judgment... In the latter situations having regard to the role the legislation gives to [the BSC]...it is something for [the BSC] to determine not the courts. The nature of their work and their membership are important when considering the role of the courts in relation to adjudications by [the BSC]. What constitutes an infringement of privacy or bad taste or failure to conform to proper standards of decency is very much a matter of personal judgment. This is not an area on which the courts are well equipped to adjudicate. (www.bsc.org.uk)

The courts have traditionally regarded the protection of privacy as a sensitive task far better suited to experts in the media industry than those who sit on the bench. The principle underlying the deference expressed by the Court is based upon belief in the expertise of the regulatory bodies concerned and, more significantly, judicial modesty as to the Court's expertise. But do such claims require expert evidence from the regulatory bodies? Or is the task of assessing infringements of privacy a task which the courts are as well placed to judge as any other body?

English law has certainly always offered piecemeal protection to many aspects of private life. Recognition for the sanctity of personal autonomy has been reflected in the development of torts in the area of confidence, defamation, trespass and nuisance. Specific enhanced protection has also been created for certain aspects of privacy by statute. Recent examples include the Protection from Harassment Act 1997 and the Data Protection Act 1998. Yet the case of *Kaye* was a clear reminder of the limitations of the protection that the law was able to offer and the case of Anna Ford highlights the reluctance of some parts of the judiciary to offer any protection.

It may come as a surprise that it is only now that lawyers in this jurisdiction may truly speak of a right to privacy, after this judgment of Lord Justice Sedley given in *Douglas, Zeta-Jones, Northern Shell plc v Hello! Ltd*.

> we have reached a point at which it can be said with confidence that the law recognises and will appropriately protect a right of personal privacy. (*Douglas* [2001])

This paper will consider how we have reached this point so suddenly, and the implications of the manner of our arrival for the right to privacy in the future.

Douglas v Hello!

On the evening of 18 November 2000, Michael Douglas and Catherine Zeta-Jones were married in New York. The marriage of two international film-stars was bound to attract the attention of the world's press and the rights to the photographs would be highly prized and costly. The wedding couple planned to benefit from that fact and so, ten days earlier, they had entered into a commercial agreement with *OK!* magazine, selling the exclusive rights to photograph the event subject to the couple's retaining wide rights of approval of the photographs to be used.

The efficacy of the agreement inevitably depended upon the prevention of other photographers from taking or using photographs of the occasion. Guests were therefore informed that they should not bring cameras to the event. Access to the reception was strictly controlled and security was imposed to prevent unauthorised cameras being taken into or used at the reception.

But the security failed. Two days after the event, the bride was told that *Hello!* magazine were proposing to publish unauthorised photographs of the reception. The bride, her groom and the company to which they had sold the exclusive photographic rights commenced urgent litigation in the English courts to injunct *Hello!* magazine from going ahead with the publication.

Perhaps in recognition of the fragility of the common law's protection of privacy, the claimants articulated their underlying causes of action for an injunction on a number of alternative bases: malicious falsehood, interference with contractual relations, breach of confidence and infringement of copyright. Their application in the High Court was initially successful. On 21 November 2000, Justice Hunt granted an injunction until trial or further order restraining *Hello!* from publishing the photographs. The defendant's appeal was heard urgently over the next two days. The Court of Appeal (Lord Justices Brooke, Sedley and Keene) allowed the appeal and discharged the injunction after the hearing.

Significantly, the marriage and reception at the New York plaza took place one month after the Human Rights Act 1998 came into full force.

The recognition of a right to privacy

Whilst the claimants' case was put in terms of breach of confidence, the Court of Appeal recorded that it was said in argument on behalf of the claimants that the case had more to do with privacy than confidentiality. This concession was critical in requiring the Court of Appeal to conduct an analysis of the law relating to privacy rather than simply an evaluation of the position based upon principles relating to the law of breach of confidence.

The concession appears to have been made because no one knew who the photographer was, a guest, an employee of a company working at the reception, or an intruder. If the photographer could have been shown to have been a guest or an employee, the Court could have more easily found that the Claimants had established the likelihood of a successful breach of confdence claim. The fact that the guests were informed by the invitation and at the reception itself that no photographs were allowed would be likely to be enough for an obligation of confidence. Similarly, the express contractual obligations imposed upon the employees coupled with their knowledge of the security arrangements would have given rise to a strong claim in confidence against an employee. The claimants had further contended that *Hello!* knew the confidential nature of the information in line with the principles espoused by Lord Goff of Chieveley in *Attorney General v Guardian Newspapers Ltd (2)* [1990].

However, the Court also recognised the possibility that the trial judge might find that the photographer was an intruder with whom no relationship of trust or confidence had been established. That possibility necessitated a cause of action which was 'not bolstered by considerations of confidence', in other words 'whether Mr Douglas and Ms Zeta Jones had a right to privacy which English law would recognise'.

All three Lords Justices conducted an analysis of the position by reference to the development of the common law, the effect upon that of the new Human Rights Act (HRA), and the right to respect for private life in Article 8 of the European Convention on Human Rights (ECHR).

Authority and obligations of the courts under the Human Rights Act

The privacy cases brought in the first years of the HRA hinged on some of the more general questions about the place of the HRA in UK law. In particular, could the HRA be used in a general way against anyone, or was it only to be used in 'vertical' cases against public authorities?

The scope of privacy rights in the HRA

In his analysis, Lord Justice Brooke considered exactly what obligations were imposed by the Human Rights Act. There exists some ambiguity in Article 8 as to the scope of privacy rights. Although Article 8(1) of the Convention in Schedule 1 to the Human Rights Act identified a right to respect for private life, the use of the words 'public authority' in Article 8(2) suggests that it appears to be concerned only with interferences with privacy by the state and not by private individuals or organisations. This had given rise to the vexed question as to whether such rights enshrined in the Human Rights Act 1998 were limited to 'vertical effect' or whether the obligations on the courts and public authorities under the Act, in conjunction with the recognition of fundamental rights and freedoms could give rise to 'indirect horizontal effect' so as to make a right to privacy enforceable against individuals within the state.

The dilemma was identified by Brooke in the following terms:

> On the one hand, Article 8(1) of the Convention appears to create a right exercisable against all the world, to respect for private and family life. On the other hand, Article 8(2) of the Convention, Section 8 of the Act, and the general philosophy of both the Convention and the Act (namely that these rights are enforceable only against public authorities), all appear to water down the value of the right created by Article 8(1).

He noted that Article 1 of the Convention has frequently been used to oblige governments to protect human rights threatened by the actions of private entities. The Article states:

> The High Contracting Parties shall secure to everyone within their jurisdiction the rights and freedoms defined in Section I of this Convention.

Although there is no clear UK statutory obligation or guidance in the Human Rights Act which guarantees to give rise to a 'horizontal right' to privacy, Brooke noted that the European Court has expressly acknowledged the positive obligations Member States have under the European Convention. The existence of a positive obligation in respect of the rights under Article 8(1) had been expressly recognised by the European Court in *X and Y v The Netherlands* in the context of the right to respect for family life. As the Court had stated:

> in addition to [the]...primarily negative obligation, there may be positive obligations inherent in an effective respect for

> family life. These obligations may involve the adoption of measures designed to secure respect for private life even in the sphere of the relations of individuals between themselves. (cited in *Douglas* [2001])

Brooke used the example of *A v United Kingdom* [1998] as a case where the Convention was found to impose positive obligations (via Article 1) on the UK to remedy deficiencies in the common law, in the absence of which the UK was held to violate the Convention. Significantly, for the purposes of Article 8(1) and the right to respect for privacy he found that the UK had 'narrowly escaped' a similar finding of failing to take positive steps of protection in the case of *Spencer v United Kingdom* [1998]. The ECHR had rejected as inadmissible a complaint regarding a photograph of Lady Spencer taken using a telephoto lens whilst she was attending a private clinic for medical treatment. The basis for the rejection was the UK's submission that Lady Spencer had failed to exhaust her domestic remedies in the UK courts by bringing an action for breach of confidence. Brooke said:

> Where Parliament in this country has been so obviously content to leave the development of the law to the judges, it might seem strange if the absence of Article 1 from our national statute relieved the judges from taking into account the positive duties identified by the court at Strasbourg when they develop the common law.

In the view of Brooke at least, the issue of horizontal effect remains a live one, which has yet to be resolved by the courts.

On the facts of the case, Brooke felt it unnecessary for the Court to decide the extent of the right and its basis. However, he was clear that the task of definition and enforcement fell clearly within the judiciary's domain and that the concern to establish and protect a right to privacy was one for which the judiciary had good credentials. Referring to the 1993 Annual Report of the Law Commission, he identified the Law Commission's concern as to the creation of a statutory tort of privacy:

> In the event the executive and the legislature took the line of least resistance and left the development of both these fields of

> law to the judiciary, and that is how matters now stand...during the last 20 years some of our most senior judges have underlined the importance of the right to privacy.

Brooke's optimism was, no doubt, affected by the existence of the Human Rights Act 1998 and the effect of the obligations (including positive obligations) on public bodies (including the courts) to act compatibly with the Convention rights, under section 6(1) and (6) of that Act. It appears that his confidence in the future protection of a right to privacy stems from the positive obligations which are deemed to flow from the Convention itself.

The need for the new right

Like Brooke, Lord Justice Keene was unwilling to say definitively that the Human Rights Act could justify the creation of a new cause of action by judicial pronouncement, given some of the limitations in the Act. Instead, Keene preferred an approach of fresh analysis of the common law and equity assisted by the impetus of the interpretative obligation under the Human Rights Act 1998:

> Already before the coming into force of the Act there have been persuasive dicta...to the effect that a pre-existing confidential relationship between the parties is not required for a breach of confidence suit. The nature of the subject matter or the circumstances of the breach and the defendant's activities may suffice in some instances to give rise to liability for breach of confidence. That approach must now be informed by the jurisprudence of the Convention in respect of Article 8. Whether the resulting liability is described as being for breach of confidence or for breach of a right to privacy may be little more than deciding what label is to be attached to the cause of action, but there would seem to be merit in recognising that the original concept of breach of confidence has in this particular category of cases now developed into something different from the commercial and employment relationships with which confidentiality is mainly concerned.' (*Douglas* [2001], per Keene)

He went on to suggest that these considerations and, in particular, the obligation to take into account the right to respect for private life under Article 8 when interpreting the common law, might well lead to the case of *Kaye* being decided differently today, particularly given the absence of any claim for breach of confidence in that case.

In the absence of a statute from Parliament, it appears that the Human Rights Act will oblige the courts to reinterpret and extend existing laws to take account of Article 8. It is as yet unclear as to whether existing laws will be deemed to provide sufficient protection, or the extent to which the courts will be able to define and protect the right to privacy.

We shall now examine the ways in which the right may be established and look at how freedom of expression can be balanced with any new right.

Development of the right to privacy

Having established that the courts could establish and protect a right to privacy, the question turned to how this new right might be developed. In the case of common law and equity, Lord Justice Sedley was quick to recognise both a virtue and a vice of English jurisprudence that depended in part on its development of such concepts:

> The common law, and equity with it, grows by slow and uneven degrees. It develops reactively, both in the immediate sense that it is only ever expounded in response to events and in the longer-term sense that it may be consciously shaped by the perceived needs of legal policy… The history of the law of confidence, however, while it displays many instances of the first kind of reactivity, has shown little of the second. The courts have done what they can, using such legal tools as were to hand, to stop the more outrageous invasions of individuals' privacy; but they have felt unable to articulate their measures as a discrete principle of law'(*Douglas* [2001], per Sedley)

Yet, Sedley concluded that equity and the common law, invigorated by the obligations of the HRA and development over time, were today in a position to respond to an increasingly invasive social environment by affirming the right 'to some private space'.

Again, the question arose as to how that right could either be rediscovered or refashioned from a common law and equity which had so strikingly refused to evolve to protect an incapacitated victim lying in a hospital bed and exposed to unwanted publicity. With a questioning glance back, Sedley suggested it would be unhelpful to ask now whether the *Kaye* conclusion would necessarily have been reached had the line of cases embodied by *Prince Albert v Strange* been argued before the Court of Appeal. His view was that the legal landscape had been altered. Yet the very nature of the common law and equity requires those changes to be mapped out and explained 'geographically'. For the right to emerge in common law and equity terms, it must have a provenance.

He identified this provenance, unsurprisingly, in the law of confidence. It was not considered necessary for a right to privacy to be explicitly recognised and stated by the courts for it to find expression in reality through the law of breach of confidence which contained all that was necessary for the protection of this right. Sedley claimed that articulation of the right in these terms was only a small step:

> I entertain no doubt that disclosure of a photograph may, in some circumstances, be actionable as a breach of confidence. If someone with a telephoto lens were to take from a distance and with no authority a picture of another engaged in some private act, his subsequent disclosure of the photograph would, in my judgment, as surely amount to a breach of confidence as if he had found or stolen a letter or diary in which the act was recounted and proceeded to publish it. In such a case the law would protect what might reasonably be called a right of privacy, although the name accorded to the cause of action would be breach of confidence. (*Douglas* [2001], per Sedley)

This passage has often been the source of academic and extra-judicial commentary and speculation as a true expression of the versatility of the common law to give effect to this right (see, for example, Bingham 1996, Singh 1998 and Neill 1999). Sedley also cited the speech of Lord Goff in *Attorney General v Guardian Newspapers Ltd (2)* [1990] in which it was indicated that protection would be afforded to cases where confidential information was obtained by a third party by chance where that information is obviously confidential.

The principle of law developed from argument on a case-by-case basis is of course fundamental to common law and equity. It is the backbone of the law's dynamic qualities and, of course, also its vice. For many domestic lawyers, the jurisprudence of the Strasbourg institutions brings with it alien concepts of legal interpretation. The organic nature of the European Convention coupled with the absence of a rigid doctrine of precedent are often seen by English lawyers as the origins of legal uncertainty and instability. Yet these concepts which enable the Convention to respond to the ever-changing needs, morals and principles of society, are also at the heart of common law and equity in a healthy domestic system. This is the advantage identified by Lord Bingham of Cornhill (Bingham 1996), of 'forging rules in the furnace of everyday human experience'. The common law and equity should be able to respond to the particular demands of the case before it and provide protection where protection is required.

As Sedley noted, the arguments of the UK government before the Commission could not in fact establish the law of England and Wales, but:

> the fact that this unanimous conclusion could emerge from a detailed consideration, after written and oral argument, of the state of the extant English authorities by a body of distinguished European jurists is of real persuasive force. It would not be a happy thing if the national courts were to go back without cogent reason on the United Kingdom's successful exegesis of its own law. (*Douglas* [2001], per Sedley)

Privacy on its own two feet

Sedley's analysis of the common law led him to the conclusion that Michael Douglas and Catherine Zeta-Jones had, at the least, a powerfully arguable case to advance at trial of rights to privacy which would be recognised and protected in appropriate circumstances. Yet in an important addition to this analysis, his Lordship sought to distinguish the notion of the breach of law of confidence as previously understood, from the right to privacy:

> What a concept of privacy does, however, is accord recognition to the fact that the law has to protect not only those people whose trust has been abused but those who simply find themselves subject to an unwanted intrusion into their personal lives. The law no longer needs to construct an artificial relationship of confidentiality between intruder and victim: it can recognise privacy itself as a legal principle drawn from the fundamental value of personal autonomy. (*Douglas* [2001], per Sedley)

This distinction between the law of confidence and the law of privacy is one which needs to be articulated and recognised. Placing a right of privacy within the law of confidence, confined within the legal strait-jacket of this label, can only damage its proper growth and development. The misplaced desire to give legal orthodoxy to the right as one which is really part of a principle that has always existed is more likely to lead to its distortion and misuse. Whilst it remains likely that the laws of confidence will influence the development of any right to privacy, we should be aware that there are lurking dangers for the right to privacy if the Court continues to articulate that right only through the law of confidence.

If, for example, the residual elements of the law of confidence still require that in any action to protect privacy, the claimant must show that the defendant knew there was some form of obligation of confidence, then the claimant may be deprived of protection merely through the reasonable ignorance of the defendant. By contrast, a right to privacy untramelled by ingredients of the law of confidence would be able to examine all the circumstances and weigh up the claimant's right to privacy as balanced against the actions of the defendant who is said to have infringed the privacy and enable the Court to provide protection where protection was due.

Can the courts balance freedom of expression and privacy?

There is a tradition of judicial deference to the media regulators. Many inside and outside the legal system believe that the delicate task of balancing media intrusion against public interest is best left to the experts. They argue that a legal remedy would impose too many limitations on legitimate reporting.

Both Lord Justice Sedley's judicial innovation and Lord Justice Keene's interpretative reappraisal accord with the general expectation that a right to privacy developed under the common law will be established in the wake of the HRA (see Singh 1998). They also accord with Parliamentary intent as reflected by the Lord Chancellor's comments to the House of Lords envisaging that the courts were free, and likely, to develop a right to privacy in the common law and that it was better that this should be done in the context of recognition of all Convention rights (including the competing right of freedom of expression under Article 10), rather than in isolation. This was readily demonstrated by the outcome of the *Douglas* case.

A synthesis of the common law, equity and the obligations under the HRA should ensure that development of the right to privacy does not proceed in a vacuum and, in particular, without having regard to the 'due high value' to be accorded to Article 10 which was of such concern to the Press Complaints Commission when the Human Rights Bill passed through Parliament (Hansard 1997).

The Court's determination as to the interim injunction in *Douglas* turned upon its analysis of Section 12 of the Human Rights Act. This important section deals expressly with the circumstances under which prior restraint of publication may be permitted. The Court had to balance the competing rights of celebrity and newspaper alike. Section 12(3) of the HRA provides that: 'No such relief is to be granted so as to restrain publication before trial unless the court is satisfied that the applicant is likely to establish that publication should not be allowed.' The effect of section 12(3) was to make prior restraint of publication of the offending material more difficult in cases where freedom of expression is concerned'. Section 12(4) introduces the requirement to have regard to any relevant privacy code[2].

When dealing with Section 12, the Court must carry out this balancing exercise while applying the concepts of legality and proportionality. There is no suggestion that the Court is either unable or less suited than others to carry out this sensitive task.

Brooke considered the new provisions of Section 12(4) of the Act, which required courts to take into account any current relevant privacy codes. In so doing, he considered the relevant Clauses of the PCC's Code of Practice:

Clause 3 of the PCC code states:

> i) Everyone is entitled to respect for his or her private and family life, home, health and correspondence. A publication will be expected to justify intrusions into any individual's private life without consent.
>
> ii) The use of long lens photography to take pictures of people in private places without their consent is unacceptable. Note – Private places are public or private property where there is a reasonable expectation of privacy.

His Lordship found the provisions so simple and easy to use that he had little difficulty in applying them to the facts of the *Douglas* case through the requirement of section 12(4) without delving into unresolved issues of torts of privacy:

> the existence of these statutory provisions, coupled with the current wording of the relevant privacy code, mean that in any case where the court is concerned with issues of freedom of expression in a journalistic, literary or artistic context, it is bound to pay particular regard to any breach of the rules set out in Clause 3 of the code, especially where none of the public interest claims set out in the preamble to the code is asserted. (*Douglas* [2001], per Brooke)

There is nothing to suggest that judges are either unable or less able to carry out an assessment of the competing rights in play in a high-profile celebrity wedding. In a 'disarmingly simple' analysis, Brooke summarised the position in a few sentences:

> So far as privacy is concerned, the case of the first and second claimants is not a particularly strong one. They did not choose to have a private wedding, attended by a few members of their family and a few friends, in the normal sense of a 'private wedding'. There is nothing in the Court's papers to belie the suggestion...of the disputed Issue 639 of *Hello!* that they invited 250 guests, and the trappings of privacy in this context

> are identical with the trappings of confidentiality to which I have alluded earlier in this judgment.

The Court decided that although the claimants were likely to establish their right to privacy at a full trial, publication of the photographs should not be prevented. All three Lords Justices concurred in discharging the injunction against *Hello!*. There was a strong balance of convenience argument for such discharge because *OK!* magazine could more readily be compensated in damages for any breach which was subsequently established at trial, whereas *Hello!* would suffer very serious consequences which would be difficult to assess financially if it were not permitted to publish its magazine. Yet it is also significant that the Court of Appeal did not feel hindered in carrying out their own balancing exercise. Not only did they not feel hindered, but each of the Lords Justices embarked upon a reasoned analysis of this balancing exercise in accordance with sound principles of Strasbourg jurisprudence, analysing the different degrees of privacy which can arise. The ability of the courts to carry out such an exercise is epitomised by Keene's pithy analysis in the *Douglas* case:

> But any consideration of Article 8 rights must reflect the Convention jurisprudence which acknowledges different degrees of privacy. The European Court ruled in *Dudgeon v United Kingdom* [1982] 4 EHRR 149 that the more intimate the aspect of private life which is being interfered with, the more serious must be the reasons for interference before the latter can be legitimate... Personal sexuality, as in that case, is an extremely intimate aspect of a person's private life. A purely private wedding will have a lesser but still significant degree of privacy warranting protection, though subject to the considerations set out in Article 8(2). But if persons choose to lessen the degree of privacy attaching to an otherwise private occasion, then the balance to be struck between their rights and other considerations is likely to be affected. (*Douglas* [2001], per Keene)

All members of the Court of Appeal attached weight to the fact that, whilst the wedding was intended to be a private occasion, the real reason for the privacy attached to the occasion was to secure the commercial rights inherent in the photographs for subsequent worldwide publication in *OK!* magazine. The major part of the claimant's privacy rights had been the subject of commercial transaction and therefore any subsequent breach if established at trial was more readily capable of financial remedy.

Whilst the Court recognised that there was a retained element of privacy in the form of the couple's reservation of editorial selection of the photographs to be published, they appeared to accept the view that this was as much a commercial as a personal reservation which could also be subject to general damages.

This pragmatic exercise of assessing competing considerations and different degrees of privacy demonstrates the Court's suitability to exercise a privacy jurisdiction and to handle comfortably the sensitive task of judging between the right to privacy and the right to freedom of expression. It is also a demonstration of the integrity of a legal right to privacy. It may be articulated and it may be protected. The courts are both able and willing to assess all countervailing considerations. As Sedley made clear, the right to privacy does not disappear in the face of commercial exploitation:

> I do not suggest for a moment that there is a bright line between the personal and the commercial and that everything on the commercial side, being about money, can be dealt with by an award of damages. Nor, equally, should it be thought that either Article 8 or our domestic law will never protect privacy which is being turned to commercial ends. Everything will depend on the infinite variety of facts thrown up case by case.(*Douglas* [2001], per Sedley)

This contextual approach should put paid to the notion that those who are cast into the public eye (for whatever reason, be it commercial, political or personal) lose their rights to privacy completely. Each case is capable of being adjudicated upon by the courts on a case by case basis within a framework which acknowledges a right to privacy but also giving due weight to the public interest in knowing about public figures.

Conclusion and challenges

Despite the fact that English judges have traditionally deferred to both the statutory and self-regulating media bodies, for the *Douglas* case the members of the Court of Appeal were not deflected from carrying out their own assessments and expressed no difficulty based on lack of expertise in dealing with this issue. As the cases of *Douglas* and *Venables and Thompson* [2001] demonstrate, the courts are as well-placed as any public body in society to adjudicate upon competing rights. There is no particular magic in the exercise. In carrying out a judicial assessment, the Court like the regulator must naturally weigh in the balance all relevant evidence. Yet it is the expertise and process of judicial assessment that arguably renders the courts rather than the regulator, better placed to fulfil the sensitive task. Accordingly, where the Court is required to carry out the sensitive task, then there is no reason why it should not continue to do so confident in its own abilities. Furthermore, many members of the public are sceptical about self-regulatory bodies such as the PCC, which is established by the media, as contrasted with statutory bodies such as the BSC.

One issue which has not been resolved is the relationship between the courts and the current regulatory bodies. As we have seen, judicial review cases, even after the Human Rights Act have fought shy of overturning decisions by the regulators. It remains an open question as to whether the Court's decision would have been different had it been considering a judicial review of the PCC. This difference of this approach to the judicial review cases mentioned earlier will need to be reconciled in due course. If the tort of privacy or a tort of breach of confidence is to emerge and flourish, then the courts will need to balance the competing rights of freedom of expression and the right to privacy more frequently. The deference accorded to the self-regulatory bodies will no longer be possible or justifiable

Once the authority of the courts is accepted, the question will turn to developing the legal concepts and tools to assess privacy issues. It is clear that the judicial recognition given to the concept of the right to privacy has reinvigorated the law of confidence. We have argued that too great an emphasis on the law of confidence would be harmful to development of a sensitive and practical right to privacy. Despite some overlap, the two concepts are different in scope and it is unlikely that the law of confidence will be able to be extended enough to deal with the subtleties of privacy regulation. A new concept of privacy is needed which incorporates ideas of what a democratic public ought to know and pays heed to freedom of expression and the circumstances in which each case arises.

Yet there remains an unsatisfactory relationship between the right to respect for private life expressed in Article 8 and the widespread anxiety on the part of the courts to express any new principle of law. If the law has now developed to recognise and protect a right to privacy, then there should be no reluctance in expressing that right in a clear and explicit way. The courts are now well equipped to define and protect that right within the context of a balanced legal system where context is everything. There is little to be feared from such a legal system. It is the legal system of the traditional common law as well as that of a modern rights-based society. The time has come to say openly that there is a right to privacy in English law.

Endnotes

1. This is a shortened version of a paper presented at an IPPR seminar on 23 January 2002. An earlier version has appeared in the *European Human Rights Law Review*.
2. The privacy codes are not specified under the HRA, in contrast to the position under the Data Protection Act 1998. There are a number of codes governing the media.

References

A v United Kingdom [1998] 27 EHRR 61

Attorney General v Guardian Newspapers Ltd (2) [1990] 1 AC 109, at 281

Bingham (1996) 'Opinion: Should there be a law to protect rights of personal privacy' *European Human Rights Law Review* 450

Byron v Johnson [1816] 2 Mer 29

Douglas, Zeta Jones and Northern Shell plc v Hello Ltd [2001] 2 WLR 992

Hansard (1997) Lord Chancellor, 24 November, cols 784-5

Kaye v Robertson [1991] FSR 62 CA

Neill B (1999) 'Privacy: A challenge for the next century', in Markesinis, BS (ed) *Protecting Privacy* Oxford University Press

Prince Albert v Strange [1849] 1 De G & Sm 652; 1 Mac & G 25

R v Broadcasting Standards Commission ex parte British Broadcasting Corporation [2000] 3 WLR 1327

Singh R (1998) 'Privacy and the media after the Human Rights Act 1998' *European Human Rights Law Review* 712

Spencer v United Kingdom [1998] 24 EHHR CD105

Venables and Thompson v Newsgroup Newpapers and Associated Newspapers Ltd [2001] 2 WLR 1038

Warren and Brandeis (1890) 'The Right to Privacy' *Harvard Law Review* 193

5. The Broadcasting Standards Commission and privacy complaints

Lord Dubs

The Broadcasting Standards Commission (BSC) has a statutory duty to consider complaints about unwarranted infringement of privacy and unfair treatment or unjust treatment by broadcasters. Its members are appointed by government, but it is independent of government and of the broadcasting industry. While some members of the Commission have media industry experience, it offers not self-regulation but independent regulation. It also offers a free and less protracted alternative to court action for someone aggrieved by broadcast material.

There are various limitations on what the Commission can do, but each of these has strong, positive consequences, rather than merely limiting its scope. In the first place, it can only deal with complaints from people directly affected by a broadcast. While this is far more relevant in limiting complaints on the allied question of unfair treatment of individuals by broadcasters, fairness and privacy issues are often closely intertwined. In any event, it provides the BSC with a helpful focus on the particular person to whom harm may have been done, rather than wider abstract questions.

The second limitation is that the BSC has no power of prior restraint over broadcast material (although it can consider aspects of the way the material was obtained when it considers a complaint about a broadcast). A broadcast must actually have happened, and have been broadcast on a service licensed in the UK, before its remit can apply. So it could not, for example, do anything in the recent, notorious instance involving covert filming of Prince William because it was never broadcast. However, this restriction happily emphasises that there can be no question of censorship or of muzzling broadcast journalists. Nor would the BSC wish it otherwise.

The third, and strong, limitation is that the BSC has no powers to fine or otherwise punish broadcasters in cases where it feels they have transgressed. In such cases its sanctions are limited to requiring the broadcasting and publication of its critical finding. This means that if it is to influence broadcasters it has to maintain high quality and authority and consistency in judgments, so that broadcasters fight hard not to be censured by the BSC and are aware of, and abide by, the good practices it recommends. The BSC is largely successful in making its limited punitive powers work. They are sufficient for broadcasters to have to take notice, and be embarrassed by them, but light enough for them to be reasonably constructive and receptive in their approach to BSC rulings.

In the year 2001, the BSC dealt with 111 fairness and privacy complaints which it found to be within its remit. Of these, only eight were exclusively concerned with unwarranted infringement of privacy; 36 involved both alleged unfairness and infringement of privacy and the remaining 61 concerned unfairness alone. These cases typically involved what might be termed 'ordinary people', which, following the Court of Appeal's judgment in the April 2000 Dixons case extends to companies as well. (That is only right and proper, given that broadcasts can have a major impact on a company's business and are often in a more powerful position than, particularly, small businesses.)

For example, the Commission recently upheld a complaint about the inclusion of intrusive footage of a driver receiving medical help with serious injuries sustained in a motorway accident which had been broadcast without his consent. While the Commission recognised the right of broadcasters to film at the scene of accidents in public places for news reporting and documentary purposes, the broadcast footage of the victim included extensive close-up shots of him receiving medical treatment from the paramedics and he was clearly identifiable. The Commission considered that he had a justifiable expectation of privacy in such circumstances and that, while the programme was justified in drawing attention to issues of road safety, this did not amount to an overriding public interest to justify using the explicit and distressing shots of the injured man.

In another case, the Commission found that a builder's privacy had been unwarrantably infringed by way of 'doorstepping' in circumstances where he had offered to give a statement and where there was no evidence of wrong-doing and therefore no overriding public interest in taking this approach.

In a third case, the Commission accepted that a documentary exposing the trade in Thai women served an important public interest.

However, it found that the programme-makers had failed effectively to disguise three young victims of the trade who had agreed to be interviewed on this sensitive subject. Since there had been no overriding public interest in identifying the three individuals, the Commission found that the broadcaster had unwarrantably infringed their privacy.

The BSC does not, of course, always uphold complaints, and it strives to be rigorously impartial between the complainant and the broadcaster. In practice, of all fairness and privacy complaints, on average, 45 per cent are upheld and in some instances the Commission partially upholds complaints. Often there is a material dispute about what actually went on in the making of a programme. In such a case, or for any other compelling reason, the BSC holds a formal, but private and non-judicial, hearing at its offices before a panel of three Commissioners, which the complainant and broadcaster attend. The proceedings are unavoidably adversarial, but the hearing seeks only to get at the facts. Not infrequently, each party genuinely achieves a better understanding of the other's perspective and a hearing can serve a useful purpose for both sides, irrespective of the outcome. This owes a lot to the skill and patience of the BSC Commissioners. Where the complaint is not upheld, the complainant still demonstrably has had their voice listened to. Moreover, even when the BSC concludes that substantive wrong has not been done, it often comments when things could have been done better, and broadcasters often admit mistakes, and overhaul procedures, in the process of preparing their case.

There are, of course, obvious limitations in only being able to act once a complaint has been made and damage has perhaps been done. The BSC seeks to keep broadcasters up to the mark by publishing and periodically revising its fairness and privacy code. This code of guidance begins with the most general principles, some of which are worth briefly stating here. They reflect both the Commissioners' experience of dealing with complaints and the Commission's research into public attitudes. Most basically of all, the code affirms that an infringement of privacy has to be justified by an overriding public interest in the disclosure of the information. Moreover, the means of obtaining the information must be proportionate to the matter under investigation. For much of the time, the private lives of most people are of no public interest. When broadcasters are covering events in public places they should ensure that the words spoken or images shown are sufficiently in the public domain to justify their broadcast without the consent of the individuals concerned. In clearly sensitive situations in places such as hospitals or prisons or police stations, individuals' consent should normally be obtained unless their identity has been concealed. Not all matters which interest the public are in the public interest. People in the public eye or their immediate family or friends do not forfeit the right to privacy, though there may be occasions where private behaviour raises broader public issues.

Following these and similar, important, general statements of principle, the code proceeds to deal with specific issues such as the use of hidden microphones and cameras, doorstepping and the treatment of children. The code is a living instrument, periodically refined in the light of practical experience in dealing with individual complaints, and of research such as the important study of the public's view of the public interest presented in Chapter 6. As that study makes clear, the very notion of what is accepted as private space changes over time. The BSC is to embark on a comprehensive overhaul of its fairness and privacy code in preparation for the advent of the integrated OFCOM regulator.

The Government has made it clear that it wishes essentially to maintain the existing BSC procedure in the new OFCOM. Indeed, in preparation for OFCOM, the BSC considers, on their behalf, complaints made to the ITC and the Radio Authority on fairness and privacy issues. The Government's stance is, of course, a welcome recognition of the fact that this piece of the regulatory machinery works. Indeed, it works primarily because it seeks to promote understanding and learn lessons, rather than to impose penalties. That being so, it should continue to serve a useful purpose, in providing free and relatively rapid remedy for aggrieved parties. It is also a system which appears to command the confidence of the broadcasting industry.

The new OFCOM will, however, require some adaptation of the existing arrangements. In particular, the merger of the BSC with the commercial broadcasting regulators will mean that the whole array of licence enforcement sanctions is available following a complaint which is upheld. The Commission will want to ensure that under the new regime it does not lose the speed, simplicity and relative informality which are the merits of the existing system. For example, the BSC would not wish hearings to become aridly adversarial and protracted. That would detract from their signal virtue as mechanisms for learning lessons and improving practice.

The BSC model is not a perfect or complete one, from the complainant's perspective. The Commission tries to ensure that the complainant's voice is fully heard and to make procedures constructive and fair, rather than daunting and formal. But it is not resourced to carry out a large-scale invigilatory or investigative operation, and of course it would fundamentally alter the nature of its work were it to do so. The Commission largely relies on the determination of complainants and the shrewdness of Commissioners to root out when things have gone wrong. However hard the BSC tries to put things right, through strengthening and publicising the code, buttressed with sanctions for the recalcitrant broadcasters, it can only cry foul after the event. Nevertheless, the Commission's (and its predecessor body the BCC) 21 years of experience of handling privacy cases has illustrated the virtues of robustly independent oversight of broadcasters. The spirit of starting from individual people's concerns, and independently upholding principles generally accepted by the public, is one which will surely be taken forward into OFCOM.

6. From 'public interest' to 'social importance': the public's view of the public interest

David Morrison and Michael Svennevig

This chapter examines how the idea of privacy has changed, and questions the concept of 'the public interest defence' as a workable ruling for judging intrusion of privacy. It draws upon interviews conducted with regulators, media personnel within radio, television, newspapers and the internet, along with media pressure groups, trade bodies and a media lawyer. In all, thirteen interviews were conducted. In addition, eight focus groups, and a national representative survey of 1039 people were used. The study was commissioned by the Broadcasting Standards Commission (BSC), BBC, Independent Television Commission (ITC), Radio Authority, ICSTIS and IPPR. The research aimed to elucidate which facts and situations people think of as private and uncover the public's view of the public interest.

The problem with public interest

The conceptual language used to discuss the adjudication of the intrusion of privacy has little analytical rigour. As a result the debate about rights to privacy has been inconclusive. The language used has difficulty in providing common ground for the resolution of claims and complaints, nor does it seem that actual practices of the media, the logic under which they operate, are sufficiently taken into account when deciding the issues of privacy.

The terms used - 'privacy', 'community of interest', and 'public interest'- are all problematic, which hampers discussion about whether individual rights to privacy must give way to the public interest. All that we have are areas, such as health, safety, military security and so on, where the defence of being in the public interest is likely to be supported. The term public interest suffers the same fate as claiming that something is in the 'national interest'. Both terms confuse as much as they clarify.

What, we must ask, constitutes the public interest? One definition of the term is that the public interest is simply whatever the public is interested in knowing. Another is that the public interest is whatever is in the interests (to the benefit) of the public to know or what the public has a right to know. Facts that are in the public interest are reported as part of the process of democratic accountability. To complicate matters futher, some would argue that there exist instances where it might be agreed that something is of public importance or interest, but that it is better for society as a whole not to reveal material in case, for example, panic ensues and undermines the efforts made by 'authorities' to protect the public from a threat. These varying definitions of 'public interest' show the difficulty of using the term as if it were a clear entity. The problem with public interest is that it is a highly political category, and for that reason lacks legal precision.

We can do no more here than give a few examples of the contentious nature of the term public interest. In the survey stage of the study, 20 per cent of the sample considered that the media coverage of the September 11th attack on the World Trade Center in New York had contained items which they felt were not in the public interest. Among this minority, leaving aside the catch-all category of 'other type of coverage', the most often-mentioned specific element of coverage felt to be inappropriate was 'pictures of people jumping out of the buildings', closely followed by 'phone calls from the victims to their families'. We do not know from the survey itself precisely why such images were not in the public interest, only that they were considered not to be.

The focus groups, however, can shed some light on this. Pictures of people jumping from the twin towers, although considered moving, frightening and powerful, were considered by many group members to be permissible images to show on the grounds of public interest. The pictures assisted the uninvolved audience in telling the story by capturing the full horror of the tragedy. Also, because the individuals could not be identified, the pictures did not give rise to considerations that privacy had been intruded upon. However, the possibility was also raised that relatives of the victims might conclude otherwise.

Matters were a little more complex with the last minute 'phone calls before death silenced those on the hijacked planes. It was considered by some that the relaying of the 'phone calls, intruded upon the privacy both of those making the calls and of those that had allowed the release of the recordings. Respondents generally agreed that these 'phone calls did not add much to the existing story in terms of capturing what had taken place. It was considered that enough information had been provided to capture the nature of the event. Even though permission had clearly been given by the relatives of the deceased to replay the messages it was considered by some that the relatives' privacy might still have been intruded upon, given that their emotional state may well have impaired rational decision-making. At issue also were questions of taste and decency. The intrusion of privacy cannot always be separated from taste and decency. We will come later to sensibilities, of what the private is taken to mean, but for the moment we wish to concentrate on the difficulty of using the term 'in the public interest' as a defence.

Political perspectives

In the focus groups the farewell messages from the stricken aircraft were considered upsetting. Let us accept that the relaying to the audience of the messages added little to the story in terms of what had taken place, but added massively to the emotional force of the drama. As such, the heart-rending broadcast of the last farewells could be expected to fuel sentiments of anger at that which had occurred. In that sense they act as good propaganda fuelling demands for military action in Afghanistan. From one political perspective, those favouring military intervention, such publication can be said to be in the public interest. From another political perspective, that military intervention might only exacerbate the problem of terrorism by creating increased bitterness towards America and thus drive more individuals into the terrorist camp, then it would not be held to be in the public interest to have emotions played upon by the publication of the messages. What, therefore, do we mean when it is claimed something is in the public interest?

News values

Because the notion of public interest is contested, it is that much easier to pass off something as being in the public interest when what we are in fact witnessing is the operation of news values, values that are derived, in large measure, from what the public is interested in. A case in point here is the news pictures of the collapse of a dance floor at a wedding in Israel, shot as it happened and showing guests happy one minute and the next falling to their death. The pictures were taken by a fellow guest at the wedding. A senior figure within ITN mentioned that, not too many years ago, cameras were hardly ever present at such an event, but now, due to the spread of camcorders and so on, much material is now on offer that would otherwise not be available. This, as we will discuss shortly, has altered the realm of the private, but for the moment let us look at news values and public interest. They are not one and the same, yet one is given justification by the other, or at least was in the case of the collapsing dance floor in talking with press, radio and television personnel.

The defence for showing what was undeniably arresting footage of the dance floor collapse, was that to do so was in the public interest, in order to show what can happen as a result of jerry-building. But this was not England, it was Israel. Unless one wishes to say that it is in the public interest for people to realise that if buildings are constructed badly there is a danger that they will collapse and kill people, then it is hard to say where the defence of public interest enters. To know the construction practices of England could be held to be in the public interest, but it is unlikely that many people would agree that knowing about the construction practices of Israel, Bolivia, or any other distant place, of vital importance to them. The interest was in the drama, and the collapse of the dance floor fulfilled a central news value of capturing the dramatic, most usually fulfilled by negative events: a dam being built is not news, a dam bursting is news. All this illustrates the difficulty of defining 'public interest' with the lack of agreement amongst the public themselves over what is in the public interest to publish.

We are not saying that the pictures should not have been broadcast, but that they could not be defended, as they were to us, in terms of public interest. This brings us full circle, what do we mean by public interest, and raises the question, by extension, as to how valuable the term is? Might it not be better to create some other term to justify the intrusion of privacy? Before addressing this, we need to consider the idea of privacy, and indeed, the idea of openness.

Changing times, changing values

Taste and decency has always been handled normatively: the manner of their discussion has been sensitive to changing values, sensitivities and behaviours. For this reason, if nothing else, the late Mary Whitehouse's organisation, the National Viewers and Listeners Association, now Mediawatch, is to be viewed as running against the mores of the times. It was not simply that she objected to certain broadcast material as immoral, or lacking in taste and decency, but objected to the social change wherein such material found a home. Television was both a reflection of objected-to social change, but also a driver of change. We might consider that television also not simply reflects changes in how the idea of the private is constructed, but has assisted in altering such constructions. The success of Channel 4's *Big Brother*, given the fact that it is found to be entertaining, says much about levels of permissible intrusion in the lives of others but may also at the same time engender acceptance of the gaze of others on private space.

In discussing the notion of privacy with senior media personnel, most agreed that ideas as to what was private had changed over time. As such it influenced their own performance. One media interviewee commented: 'I'm sure it's [the idea of privacy] changed', and by way of explanation added: 'If you're in a public gathering of some sort, like a wedding, it's almost certain someone's filming you'. In similar vein, in the focus groups repeated reference was made to CCTV cameras, together with general acceptance of these surveillance devices. Modern complex societies can rightfully be referred to as surveillance societies, from the collection of visual images of individuals, to the electronic storage of data on the individual, especially financial data. Thus, rather than talk in terms of a right to privacy, it is perhaps more useful to talk in terms of expectations of privacy.

Space and expectations of privacy

In examining where and under what circumstances people felt that others should not intrude into their lives, it became clear that people talked in spatial terms. We discerned three basic forms of space: closed public space, restricted public space and open public space. The first, closed public space, was that bounded by the home and in that sense was not public at all. The second, restricted public space, included the neighbourhood where they lived, the office or workplace and areas such as secluded beaches or sheltered picnic spots. The third, open public space, included town centres, shopping malls and exposed beaches.

The expectation of intrusion was inversely related to the degree of openness. Thus, there was absolute expectation that performances in the home would not be open to inspection by others, through to open public space where absolute expectation existed that performance would be open to inspection. This can be explained by reference to self-monitoring. We all self-monitor that which we are doing with varying degrees of consciousness. It is helpful here to think of 'front stage' and 'back stage' performances. In a shopping centre we know we are operating front stage, whereas picnicking by some stream is back stage of a performance. We do not expect to be observed and, therefore, do not guard our performances.

The nature of publication

This division of space into expectations of surveillance must, however, as it relates to intrusion of privacy, take into account people's expectations of publication, or rather, the nature of publication. To be captured in open public space by CCTV cameras was of no bother whatsoever: it was closed and not open publication. Neither did being caught in an open public space by a television camera or a press photographer matter providing one did not have an individual biographical presence. To be part of a crowd at some premier league match was of no concern, but to be a face in the crowd was. One member in the focus groups gave an instance of his friend being shown in a lingering TV close-up, crying when his beloved Arsenal lost a game. What came across is that, although a football match is open public space and therefore one's presence could be captured as part of a general presence, to single an individual out for attention was wrong. Thus, to feature the individual in such a way, even in open public space, requires some defence.

Imprecision

A senior figure within the pressure group Presswise considered that newspaper editors do not wish for a precise definition of 'public interest', since without precision, editors are left relatively free in their operations. The lack of definition was, he considered, 'quite deliberate'. While there is no need to accept this as a motivating factor in the lack of a precise definition of public interest, it undoubtedly favours the construction of a defence when claims are lodged that a person's privacy has been wrongfully intruded upon. Throughout the research, in interviews with media personnel and regulators, in the focus groups, and in the national survey findings, it is plain that there is no universally agreed definition of the term 'public interest'.

In both the focus groups and the survey, we asked respondents directly to say what they understood by the term 'public interest'.

Over 90 per cent of the sample did offer a definition in their own words of what they understood by 'public interest' in this context, demonstrating that the broad term at least is recognised, even if it is not particularly clearly or consistently articulated.

These verbatim replies were then inspected and content-analysed into broad categories. The categorisation focused upon the underlying rationale of the definitions given by the sample and up to two different categories were coded for each. There was no clear definition to be found in the sample's definitions. Rather, there were disparate categories of themes, shown in Tables 6.1 and 6.2, together with examples of each category.

Table 6.1 Definitions of public interest: *objective*

Public rights (34%)
It's information that the public has the right to know.

Something going on needs to be brought to the public's notice.

Government officials should be accountable for their mistakes, the public should be aware of this. There are certain issues that the public should be made aware of, this is what 'public interest' means.

That it's important for people to know about what's going on in the world and for them to make informed decisions and opinions.

To make things common knowledge.

Public effects (28%)
Issues that affect ordinary people directly.

Something affecting others rather than just that person.

If it's important to other people and it is likely to affect or harm other people.

If it would affect you as a member of the public like war, disasters or floods.

Where the issue has a direct effect on people's lives.

National interest (3%)
If it's to do with the security of the country – deviousness by politicians – that sort of thing.

Something basically important, in the national interest or the people at large.

General public as a whole, all 60 million of us.

In case of danger to the public or the country and national security.

What it means is security of the country. If [a popular singer] is wearing pink knickers that's not important to the country, but if she was a spy, that is in public interest, national security.

The largest proportion of the replies (34 per cent of the sample) fell into the category we have called 'public rights'. A defining feature of this category is the use of imperative terms – 'needs', 'rights', 'should', and so on – used in support of the principle of public, democratic rights to information.

The next largest category of definitions – public effects – centres around the issue of effects and impacts. Essentially, the argument is that large-scale effects on the public at large are a priori a matter of concern.

Table 6.2 Public interest definitions: *subjective*

Interests of the public (15%)
Some news like war news and New York towers information is interesting. Good for people to know and we can discuss it with friends.

Things that the public would be interested in hearing about, celebrities' and politicians' private lives.

Anything the public would be interested in reading about.

Kind of what people are interested in reading about, what people want to see or read.

Giving the public what they want.

Personal interests (7%)
[Public interest] is not easy to define, some subjects may be of interest to some members of the public and others may be not.

Something that is going to interest you or benefit you.

Only way would be a paedophile situation because that would affect me, it would be in my interest to know as I have children.

If it doesn't affect us we don't need to know.

If it's going to affect you.

Local/community interest (2%)
Nowadays people often don't know their neighbour, so they need to know what is going on in their neighbourhood to protect themselves. The local papers, news etc does this, this is 'public interest'

Relevant to particular sections of society.

If there is a local crime or paedophile in the area, anything like that.

What is happening within your local area.

The people in the community should know what's going on if it affects them.

A second grouping of replies (Table 6.2) illustrates clear confusion for some people between the more abstract concept of the public interest as a form of public good and the specific interests of members of the public, either *en masse* or as individuals. These replies hinge around public interest being defined by the opinions and interests of the media consumer, rather than taking the more abstract form demonstrated by the replies in Table 6.1 above. Within this broad grouping of interest-led definitions are three distinct divisions into the 'public', 'personal' and 'community' levels.

Table 6.3 Public interest definitions: *based on media practice*

Unwarranted intrusion (16%)
Just like to be nosy. Not always in public interest. Good reporting shouldn't be intrusive.

I think they want to be nosy, delve into people's private lives.

Anything you think of, there is anything in public interest. I think due to public interest, newspapers take advantage to expose privacy of the person.

Public interest means that some of the things that come out will be detrimental to the people involved. Sometimes they don't have the facts right.

It's just gossip, and telling people what they think they want to hear.

Media excuse (12%)
Statement media use to absolve them of all sin. Carte blanche because they say it's public interest.

They are still just trying to sell their newspapers saying it's public interest.

Public interest is just a way of broadcasting what media want.

It's a catch-all term that gives the media carte blanche to do what it likes.

Public interest is when they get a story and make some money out of it.

Warranted intrusion (5%)
Anything that people are interested in, particularly in other people's lives, particularly celebrities and such like, just human instinct to be nosy, particularly if it is not good.

> If the matter of the subject transcends or supersedes the individual's right to privacy.
>
> I think, have a right to know what famous people get up to as people i.e. children look up to them. The politician found out doing dodgy deals etc, the public have a right to know.
>
> You know the full character of the person involved, whether they're entirely honest and reliable.

There is a further set of definitions (Table 6.3) which again reflect a different understanding of the public interest concept. These are basically formulated as observations of media practice, rather than reflections upon what form the ideal might take. Two of the categories are unreservedly critical: the media intrude for the 'wrong' reasons (unwarranted intrusion); and 'public interest' is simply a convenient cover term used by the media for the media simply doing whatever they want (media excuse).

A third subset of these replies (warranted intrusion) show that media intrusion can be part of the public interest, though again defining the concept more by actions rather than principles.

These verbatim definitions given by the sample show the lack of a common, shared definitional base for the term 'public interest'. This conclusion is reinforced by considering the fact that this question was preceded by others which did raise the general issues of public interest, these replies were not given *in vacuo*.

Nevertheless, in deciding whether or not the media had a right to intrude upon privacy, notions that approximate to what regulators mean by public interest did come to the fore. Both in the focus groups and in the survey, the idea of the generalised self is there, as also is the idea that for something to be in the public interest it had to involve the well-being of a collection of people. For our sample, the public interest is in play when the importance of collective well-being outstrips any expectations on the part of an individual, organisation or agency that their lives or performances were of their concern only. People other than themselves had good reason in knowing what they were doing, or had done.

In order to concretise the question of public interest then in both the focus groups and in the survey a scenario was created to have respondents judge whether or not the story constructed was in the public interest. Further, respondents were asked what methods were permissible by journalists in covering the story and whose privacy they could reasonably intrude upon in the course of this. Again, for the sake of conciseness we will give the findings from the survey only.

Table 6.4 The NHS scenario

A senior manager in the NHS has issued a secret instruction telling doctors that they must not use an expensive new drug treatment on older patients suffering from cancer and can only give them cheaper and less effective drugs. Some doctors are obeying this instruction, but others are disobeying it. The media want to report this story.

	Definitely yes %	*Yes* %	*No strong view* %	*Probably not* %	*Definitely not* %
First, is this an issue that should be covered by the media?	84	12	2	1	*
Would you say that this is an issue that is in the public interest?	85	13	1	1	*
Would you personally be interested in this issue?	74	16	5	4	1

The next step was to ask people which of a wide range of possible methods were acceptable means for the media to obtain the information needed to cover this story. The list used was the same as that used in the focus groups, with a few minor wording changes to suit the survey setting.

The results show a clear demarcation between a limited number of tactics thought acceptable for information-gathering and others which were thought unsuitable by majorities of the sample (Table 6.5). The methods thought appropriate include basic journalistic techniques: interviewing or telephoning those concerned at the workplace, and the affected patients and their relatives. The use of 'leaked' information was also deemed acceptable by the majority.

Those techniques thought to be unsuitable by majorities included all of the covert methods listed, such as disguised reporters, hidden cameras, searching rubbish. Illegal strategies such as 'phone-tapping and mail and e-mail interception were approved by minorities. It might have been expected that CCTV material might be regarded as beyond the pale, but this is clearly believed by most to be a legitimate source of material.

Table 6.5 Ways of getting information

There are a number of different ways in which journalists and programme-makers might be able to get information. In this particular case, the media would try to get information about the senior manager who is responsible for the order on drugs. For each of the different ways of getting information, how acceptable is it to use it in *this particular case*.

	very	*fairly*	*not very*	*not at all*	*don't know*
Interviewing relatives of elderly patients affected by the decision	41	35	12	11	2
Interviewing elderly patients affected by the decision	40	31	13	14	2
A reporter telephoning person's office	36	39	13	10	2
Using security camera pictures from office	28	37	16	15	3
Reporters waiting outside office	24	47	15	12	2
Interviewing person's work colleagues	18	46	17	16	3
Using 'leaked' information from anonymous sources	17	43	20	17	4
Hidden microphone at person's office	14	28	28	28	2
Hidden TV camera at person's office	14	27	30	27	2
Reporter at office disguised as someone else	13	33	27	25	2
A reporter telephoning person's home	12	32	24	30	2
Hidden photographer at person's office	12	29	30	27	2
A reporter telephoning person's office pretending to be someone else	11	29	29	29	2
Going through office rubbish for relevant documents	10	28	27	32	3
Reporters waiting outside person's home	8	28	27	35	2
Tapping office telephone line	8	22	25	42	2
Interviewing person's adult friends and family	7	26	28	37	2
Intercepting office email	7	23	25	41	4
Intercepting post at person's office	7	17	30	42	3
Going through person's home rubbish bins for relevant documents	6	16	31	45	2
Hidden TV camera outside person's home	6	16	30	47	1
A reporter telephoning person's home pretending to be someone else	6	12	31	50	1
Hidden photographer outside person's home	5	19	30	44	2
Intercepting home email	4	8	36	58	5
Tapping home telephone line	3	8	24	63	2
Interviewing person's children	1	3	16	78	2

One important point of principle does emerge from these findings: the home is seen as a protected place. In this particular scenario, it is abundantly clear that for most people, the professional responsibility of the NHS official to answer for his or her decisions does not extend outside the workplace. This distinction can be clearly seen in the contrast (Table 6.6) between identical methods in the work and home contexts, where the levels of approval for the home-focused methods are far lower than for their office-focused equivalents. Above all, the manager's children are effectively sacrosanct.

Table 6.6 Work versus home

	% saying very or fairly acceptable
A reporter telephoning the person's office	76
A reporter telephoning the person's home	44
Reporters waiting outside office	71
Reporters waiting outside person's home	36
Interviewing person's work colleagues	64
Interviewing person's adult friends and family	33
Interviewing person's children	4

These results closely mirror the findings from the focus groups. There are clear 'rules of engagement' operating here. However, the precise application of these rules must be assumed to be unique to this particular scenario and the particular circumstances it encompasses. If the scenario changes, the ways in which rules are applied or become capable of variation, even abandoned, will also change. Certainly, had this scenario been about severe medical malpractice, or about drug dealing or child abuse, there is little doubt that the patterns of acceptability found would be strikingly different from those seen in this case.

Public and interest

What we see in the above case and from the focus groups, is that something that affects numbers of people is construed as being sufficiently important for intrusion, of some degree, to be warranted. This judgment of when privacy can be intruded upon is right to call public interest, but what cannot be avoided, as Tables 6.1 to 6.3 – and also the groups – show, is that confusion over the term itself does exist. In light of this, it is our considered opinion that some new term might be more appropriate in clarifying the defence of intrusion, or at least form the basis for discussion.

A new term

The term 'social importance' appears to us to capture all that 'in the public interest' refers to without the operational difficulties of the latter. At a stroke, it gets rid of the troublesome referent, the public, and the cognitively bothersome word, interest.

The term 'social importance' opens judgment of intrusion to reason in a way that is not so readily the case with the term in the public interest. What, for example, is the social importance of a picture of a female newsreader sunbathing on a holiday beach? In other words, in what way can it be said that not to see such a picture, not to possess such 'knowledge', would have repercussions on how we negotiate our lives. The term, social importance can, furthermore, be graded in a way that is not very meaningful in the case of public interest. The term public interest has a gravity attached that makes it a too severe a test for intrusion of privacy. It has little sensitivity whereas social importance can be scaled from very high social importance to very low social importance. Once the level of social importance is understood, it then follows that the degree of intrusion considered to be appropriate is dependent upon that importance. It is almost arithmetic. The flexibility of the term as a workable concept means that it can handle the different types of performance expected from different types of media. That is, the notion can take account of the logic of media performances in a way that the more quasi-legal concept, public interest, cannot.

Social importance

We have drawn the notion of social importance at the empirical level from how issues of privacy were discussed in the focus groups. Members of one of the focus groups involving 30-45 year-old Leeds women defined public interest as: 'If it's going to affect you personally';. 'if it's going to affect everybody'; 'about things that happen to change your life'; or having to 'affect a good proportion of the population'. Even the woman who mentioned that for something to be in the public interest had to affect you 'personally' clearly considered that what was personal to her would be important to others, because of shared similar conditions. Although much confusion was apparent in giving definitions of the public interest, the idea of importance, or of 'things that happen to change your life', was paramount, as was the precedence of society and commonly-held societal values over the individual. Time and again in the focus groups, people judged intrusion into privacy, the degree and the methods, by the degree to which they saw behaviour as attacking the core values of our society and therefore posing a threat to social association. This was manifested in discussing a wide range of examples of wrong-doing: each was effectively graded in terms of the threat that it posed to social organisation.

Furthermore, the notion of 'social importance', drawn from ideas of social solidarity, is preferable to 'public interest' in that it is based on moral judgment and so offers the possibility of handling moral outrage in a way that public interest cannot so readily achieve. This brings the beliefs of others into the fold of intruding into privacy, on the grounds that those beliefs might constitute a threat to social solidarity.

Conclusion

The idea of social importance as a defence for the intrusion of privacy, and the ability to grade the degree of social importance, cuts away at the specious reasoning that is often presented as a justification for intruding into privacy. It also can handle what we might wish to know, but do not necessarily need to know. Social solidarity is assisted, to a degree, by the circulation of information that gives a feeling of belonging, of attachment to the world of others and acting as conversational points between people. The documentation of the lives of celebrities does just that. However, such documentation would have to ensure that the degree of intrusion into someone's private life against their wishes, would be minimal: to establish a public interest for such intrusion is to suggest importance where no importance exists. The concept of the public interest is both too clumsy and too grand to capture the operations of the media.

7. Regulating the trade in secrets: policy options

Damian Tambini and Clare Heyward

The contributions to this report have indicated the intensity of debate that surrounds the issue of privacy protection and media intrusion in UK law and regulation. Those who feel that their privacy has been violated by journalists claim that the system of privacy protection has failed. They see in the confusion following the introduction of the Human Rights Act (HRA) the opportunity for modernising protection of privacy. Their opponents see a danger that the great UK tradition of veracious investigatory journalism is threatened by a creeping regulatory approach to press intrusion. For these reasons the Press Complaints Commission has robustly represented the interests of the press in opposing the privacy provisions of the HRA at every stage in its development. In this volatile situation the new integrated communications regulator OFCOM will be developing its approach to privacy, and a new code of practice.

The policy challenge is to take an overview of the various forces at work and ask whether there is a call for regulatory or government action at this juncture, and if so, what the various agencies in the picture should consider. The policy recommendations we make in this chapter are directed at regulatory agencies, both statutory and self-regulatory, and government. We are not concerned therefore with specifying for every possible case the appropriate balance between freedom of expression, privacy and the public interest. Those balancing decisions are based on subjective and contested notions and best done on a case by case basis. We do make suggestions regarding appropriate codes of practice which are relevant to those operated by the BSC, the PCC and also the NUJ.

The policy recommendations made here are concerned with the appropriate legal and regulatory structure for dealing with these issues, and the broader impact of privacy regulation on journalistic practices, our culture, the actions of public figures and also the overall regulatory burden of conflict and uncertainty in this field. In this conclusion we argue that the current confusion about privacy rights has in some ways been constructive, but that the the time is right to outline the terms of a new settlement. We present some general principles for privacy protection and some points that OFCOM should consider in developing its approach.

The contributors to this volume outline a wide range of opinions that are the responsibility of each author. There are some very marked disagreements between these leading experts. In this chapter we develop some of them further, particularly the idea that the notion put forward by Morrison and Svennevig that the public interest is a problematic concept that has created long-term difficulties in the UK approach to media and privacy.

What is privacy?

Although this is not the place to resolve fundamental questions about the notion of privacy, we do need to know a little about this contested term in order to begin to consider appropriate regulation. Countries around the world have grappled with the subtle balances to be struck in relation to the harms to dignity associated with breaches of privacy. They have all found different solutions in balancing the need to prevent harm whilst guaranteeing the democratic freedom of the media. In German law, for example, privacy rights derive from a more general right to personality (see Neill 1999).

Certainly, the complexity of law is such that policy frameworks cannot simply be transposed from one situation to another. Comparative law can inform us of the possible frameworks available and of the various interpretations of the European Convention on Human Rights. Comparison and research can also enlighten us regarding the nature of privacy itself and the extent to which there is a workable consensus on the boundaries of the private lives to be protected. Where there is a clear and agreed notion of the limits of a private sphere, regulation could be relatively categorical about its protection. The problem faced by regulation in this sphere, however, is that there is not. Regulators have to deal with subjective, contested notions of privacy, which – as Warren and Brandeis (1890) noted in their classic treatment of privacy rights – 'change according to the long-term shifts in civilisation and culture'. Currently there is some consensus that the following concepts should form part of the definition of privacy. An exhaustive definition is, however, impossible.

Space

David Morrison and Michael Svennevig's research shows that the home is considered to be the most private area, the place for family life. Their findings are supported by historians who have mapped the rise of the public-private distinction over the past few centuries (see Weintraub and Kumar 1997). However, these subjective public perceptions are extremely difficult to incorporate into a legal and regulatory framework that offers certainty both to journalist and public figure regarding just when the threshold to the private sphere is being breached, and where there is a reasonable expectation of privacy.

Many of the difficult regulatory and legal decisions about privacy hinge on whether certain spaces (such as restaurants, beaches, gardens) can be considered private. Where courts and regulators have attempted to base decisions and guidelines on space, there have been difficulties. The German Appeal Court's opinion that the public's interest ended 'at the doorstep' was qualified by an acceptance that there are cases where there is a legitimate interest in material gathered in the home. There is also a danger inherent in spatial definitions of effectively imprisoning public figures in their own homes. We do not want to be ruled by recluses. Most would support the view that individuals should be permitted a private area worthy of protection outside that of the purely domestic.

Subject matter

Intimate relationships, medical records and financial details are all considered to be totally private and not for disclosure without permission. Intimate details of relationships, information about families, especially about school-age children should not appear in the media unless these are absolutely integral to a story. There is agreement, however, that financial details should not receive the same degree of protection. Financial arrangements are frequently at the heart of any public interest story, so it is likely that too many legitimate stories could be quashed if financial details were subject to the same protection as family and relationships. Breach of Confidence and Data Protection offer some protection in this area, but fail to deal with the issues at stake entirely.

Expectation

Both in the case of breach of confidence cases, and in cases where there is a reasonable expectation of privacy, there is a notion that our opinions about an act or a situation can influence our rights to protection. The case of Geoff Peck whose attempted suicide was caught on CCTV footage and then broadcast is relevant. His claim to privacy, which was upheld by both the BSC and the ITC, was based on an expectation that his privacy would be respected though the act was committed in a public place. As Singh and Strachan note, breach of confidence has often been used as a means to claim privacy protection, but it has been necessary to have a way of constructing real or implied prior agreement in order to establish that breach.

Point of view

This partial survey, drawn from legal and regulatory argument about what constitutes a breach of privacy, serves to illustrate the complexity of notions of privacy. The term is also very subjective. People's views of the scope of privacy vary especially according to age and perceptions of what is private will continue to change. It is the role of regulators, and occasionally the courts, to achieve balance on questions of the degree of breach and to ensure that professional journalists enjoy some degree of certainty about their rights and responsibilities (Tomlinson 2002). Research has also found significant differences between ethnic groups regarding the definitions of privacy and private space (see Chapter 6). A legal definition too closely based on clear codification of space, subject or expectation will need to be open to constant updating based on research and public involvement. Otherwise regulators will appear outdated and irrelevant.

What is publicity?

The converse of these definitions of what is private is the discussion of what constitutes publicity. As the Calcutt Committee (1990) has noted, there are two distinct moments in the violation of privacy by journalists. One is the moment of contact between the journalist and her target, and the other is the moment of publication of information considered private. Harassment and trespass law can be used against the former in some, though by no means all, cases, whilst the harm associated with publicity is less easily covered by existing law.

In the decades since Warren and Brandeis's article, we have had a keen awareness that, as Singh and Strachan put it in this volume, we live in an 'increasingly invasive social environment'. As we noted in the introduction, technological and market change have upset existing notions of the nature of publicity. Whilst it is simple to note that the degree of harm should be roughly equivalent to the extent of publicity, this depends on case-by-case variations. Current rapid growth in new media and globalisation challenge existing paradigms of regulation based on delivery technology. Regulators have to develop guidelines reflecting the 'harm' caused by publication on a little visited but easily searchable website and that caused by a mass, but momentary broadcast.

Doubt and lack of clarity is the enemy both of privacy and of press freedom. For when there is doubt about their rights, journalists and editors are less likely to take risks and there could be a chilling effect on investigations. This does not appear to be the case yet, but would be the case were courts to embark on a more thoroughgoing experiment in privacy protection. Where rules are unclear, risk will be taken in line with the financial benefits of intrusive behaviour. Where there is doubt and uncertainty for public figures on the other hand they are more likely to modify their behaviour, avoid public spaces and be more private in their communications. This, surely, is already the case.

Who has the right to privacy protection?

Morrison and Svennevig's survey reveals a range of public opinion about who can avail themselves of privacy protection and when. Aside from the legal debate about whether UK law actually recognises a right to privacy that has raged since the adoption of the HRA, there is a longer-term debate about when an individual gives up privacy rights, for example through seeking publicity.

Publicity seekers

At present, a commonly-held view is that people who have used the media in the past have surrendered their rights to privacy. A host of PCC rulings – most recently its rejection of Vanessa Feltz's complaint against the *Sunday Mirror* and the *Mirror* who had published some intimate details about her relationship with her boyfriend (corroborated by that boyfriend) – make this clear.

> The Commission has made clear on a number of occasions that it will take into account the extent to which similar matters have been discussed by the complainant or have been published before without complaint. Privacy is a right which can be compromised and those who talk about their private lives on their own terms must expect that there may be others who will do so, without their consent, in a less than agreeable way.(www.pccc.org.uk)

This view has the virtue of simplicity, but is still problematic. Voluntary disclosure of some private facts should not entail a complete waiver of the right to privacy. A person may disclose some details of her private life to her friends, or to her work colleagues. This is seen as part of everyday life, and does not permit those people to demand or seek out more information, say by reading her diary. There are degrees to privacy violations. Celebrities and politicians, by their virtue of their careers, choose to have a lesser degree of privacy than most. It will vary between people in the public eye: Victoria Beckham is seemingly content with a low degree of privacy, whereas other celebrities guard their family life very carefully and talk predominantly about their working lives in interviews. A person can choose at which level of privacy they are comfortable. However, if that person is happy to talk about some aspects of their private lives, this still does not justify declaring that every part of their life can be laid bare. Speaking to the press at one point in one's life should not be taken as 'seeking publicity' for the whole of one's life, though that is how the principle is often understood. The tendency for self-regulatory authorities to bend the rules in favour of publication in cases such as this only serves to cast further doubt on the system of self-regulation.

Public figures

In US courts, there is in effect a separate regime for public figures, including government officials and those who hold public office. It is considered reasonable that the public has a stronger interest in knowing private information about these figures, though in ways proportional to the public function they hold. In the UK, by contrast, we rely on a broader and flexibly-interpreted notion of the public interest to determine when journalists can legitimately intrude into privacy. As a consequence, public figures perhaps live in more fear of more indiscriminate media intrusion in Britain. Whilst this might offer schadenfreude to some members of the public, it will make public service less attractive and arguably expands the appetite for prurient detail.

Role models?

In practice it is difficult to maintain the boundaries between public figures and public officials, however. The recent case of *A v B and C* [2002] for example concerned the case of a footballer. Although there would have been no real justification of publication of his identity in terms of a 'public official' doctrine, the judge in the case argued for a very broad interpretation, based on the notion that he was a role model for youngsters and therefore that his infidelities should be exposed. (Whether this makes the sportsman likely to be copied in bed as well as on the football pitch by adoring youngsters was not explored.)

Inequality of access to privacy protection

Whereas there is a strong argument for a regulatory system that does permit distinction between different categories of journalistic targets, privacy protection should not depend on ability to pay. The debate about the impact of the HRA in the UK approach to privacy has focused on whether the Act creates a two-tier system with the courts providing a solution for the rich and lower levels of protection afforded by the PCC. It is probably too early, and there have been too few cases, to ascertain whether this fear is justified, but this is certainly a situation to avoid. If a second route to privacy protection was opened for those with the resources, this would entail an additional problem of double jeopardy, with courts and regulators potentially played off one against the other.

The public interest

In broad terms, journalistic intrusion can be justified in the UK, and complaints against it overturned, if the journalist successfully claims that they were breaching privacy 'in the public interest'. However, views regarding how to define the public interest that would justify intrusion cover a broad range of interpretations by the courts, by regulators and by the public. At one end of the continuum there is support for a very broad generalised 'media watchdog' role which would include what the code of the Broadcasting Standards Commission calls the need to reveal or detect 'disreputable behaviour'. At the other end, there are attempts to define the notion of public interest more narrowly in terms of the range of issues considered to warrant justifiable intrusion.

There is also an ever-present danger of fudging the notion of the 'public interest' as 'anything that the public is interested in'. Although the PCC and others regularly indicate that they do not subscribe to such a broad view, this notion of the public interest is surprisingly often in play in decisions both by regulators and the court. This problem of definitional confusion is proving endemic, with a detrimental impact on journalistic ethics[1].

Morrison and Svennevig's research shows that members of the public have an understanding of the type of story that they think is in the public interest when they are given an explanation of the term, but that the term itself is ambiguous. Members of the public were perfectly able to give reasons why a story that intruded on an individual's privacy might be justifiably reported. Put crudely, stories that have a great impact on many people's lives should be reported, even if they are intrusive. Morrison and Svennevig suggest that given the confusion regarding the 'public interest' and the potential for fudging, it would be justified to replace the term with the term 'social importance'.

The suggestion is attractive but is difficult to translate directly into policy. An obvious implication would be that codes of practice and the relevant legislation should refer to the notion of social importance rather than public interest. However, notions of 'social importance' could turn out to be just as slippery as the term they criticise. It would be extremely difficult to reach agreement on whether or not a story has a great impact on peoples lives. In particular it is doubtful whether a single central definition of matters of social importance would be justifiable.

For Morrison and Svennevig, social importance is linked to people's deeply-held moral beliefs and view of the world around them. If an issue could be considered to have an impact on the way people reflected on their lives, then it could be said to have a degree of social importance. For example, a tragedy such as the collapse of a building where a wedding was taking place and the reflections and emotions reporting it would produce might make it count as being socially important, even to people outside the country in which it occurred. Seeing a picture of a newsreader on holiday probably would not.

Whilst nearly everyone agrees that newspapers should report on stories such as mismanagement of public money, corruption or abuse of parliamentary procedure, it is less obvious that 'public interest' defends publishing details about say a politician's family difficulties. For example, some members of the public would be of the opinion that an elected official's tendency to cheat at golf, or on her husband might be relevant to her ability to run for public office. Others would disagree. Even where the former are in a minority, it would be difficult to support the argument that their right to receive relevant information should be inhibited, particularly in the case of elected officials.

> To put it differently, in a democracy there appears to be a right to base one's voting decisions on criteria that other people take to be wrong. (Schauer, cited in Neill 1999)

This argument is attractive but would be unworkable as a general guidance rule. Even if I want to base my voting intention on the colour of candidates' underwear, that would not justify journalists intruding to ensure that I receive the information I need to make my decision. It seems that despite the particular terminological confusion caused by the notion of the public interest, the job of defining justifiable intrusion into privacy cannot be resolved by a quick definitional fix. 'Public interest' is a widely-used term that appears in many sectors of regulation where regulators are given wide discretion. It is only in the case of privacy regulation that it springs a semantic trap. The answer is not to introduce a new term, it should be to better the criteria for determining the public interest more tightly. The judgment in the case of *A v B and C* suggests that some judges are in danger of making the same mistakes that the PCC frequently made in the past by reducing the public interest to whatever some members of the public happen to be interested in.

Law, regulation and privacy: Who regulates?

The bodies currently responsible for ensuring that journalists respect privacy are the PCC, the BSC and the courts. The National Union of Journalists also operates a code of practice.[2]

Regulation of the press has been a difficult and much-debated issue for much of the 20th century. So far, a system of self-regulation has been preferred, above the options of creating a tort of privacy, and creating a statutory body to oversee the press. In broadcasting, the creation of a statutory body, firstly the Broadcasting Standards Council, and later the Broadcasting Standards Commission was uncontroversial, and this system appears to have worked well.

The press has always argued vigorously for self-regulation, claiming that newspapers must be free from the control of government statute if democracy is to be best served. The Press Complaints Commission's Code of Practice was drawn up by journalists, and the Commissioners who adjudicate include a sizeable minority of newspaper editors. The advantages of this system are numerous. In particular it has buy-in from the industry, and the complaints procedure is informal, inexpensive, and free from any Orwellian overtones. Self-regulatory systems are sometimes alleged to be more effective as they secure greater co-operation from the industry. Self-regulation is also attractive politically. A consistent theme of this government, as with its predecessor, has been to reduce regulatory burdens on all types of business.

Privacy of course is only one aspect of press ethics and self-regulation; the question of the effectiveness of self-regulation also applies to issues such as fairness, accuracy and so forth. Regrettably, the debate about press self-regulation has become rather stale. The most vehement proponents of self-regulation for the press have a tendency to equate any suggestions for reform as a threat to press freedom, democracy itself and, occasionally, the world as we know it. It has been argued that a statutory body to deal with complaints is tantamount to government licensing and approval of newspaper content, despite the fact that broadcasters are regulated by statute but do not have government censors in their newsrooms. In fact, the fresh debate on self-regulation might be an incentive for the press as a whole to improve its performance. Broadcast news commands far greater respect amongst the British public, and the BBC – the most regulated of the broadcasters – is respected worldwide because it is not dictated to by government. According to the Eurobarometer poll, the UK press is trusted less than the press of any EU country, whilst our broadcasters are trusted more. Germany and Sweden have statutory regulations for the press but still manage to maintain good democratic credentials.

The same attitude pervades responses to the few injunctions granted. Justice Jack's judgment in *A v B and C* was widely denounced as an attack on press freedom and, by extension, democracy. It is sometimes forgotten that the real reason a democracy needs a free press is to enable public access a wide range of opinions about key issues, in order for citizens to evaluate and criticise their government's decisions. Many papers over the past have abused their privileges. The fight for a free press, still ongoing in many countries has been about this key function, not about the right to publish photos of celebrities on holiday, or supply an insatiable market for gossip.

The contributions to this volume make clear that the debate about the role of courts, self-regulatory authorities and statutory authorities is set to continue. They also make clear that the HRA is exerting pressure on the PCC and other authorities to improve their performance with respect to privacy. It is clear to self-regulatory authorities that where they fail to deliver privacy protection under their code, recourse could be had to the courts. There have been questions about the conduct both of the courts and of the PCC with respect to privacy protection in recent years, but some competition between them, if it does not result in too much confusion among professionals and the public, will not be a bad thing.

Summary

Since the introduction of the HRA, our system for regulating journalistic intrusion into privacy has been open to the following criticisms:

- Confusion: for journalists, the public and the public figures over when privacy should be protected, and when breach is in the public interest.

- Inadequate protection: breach of confidence and other legal remedies do not offer adequate protection in all cases.
- A tendency for self-regulatory authorities to fudge the public interest
- Inequality of protection
- Inappropriate expertise in courts
- Regulatory capture
- Two tiers of regulation, leading to confusion and double jeopardy, caused by the introduction of the HRA

Reform of privacy protection in the UK: the principles

In the context of the formation of codes for OFCOM, and future thinking on press self-regulation, the following principles for privacy protection should be taken into consideration. The first are general principles that apply across the regulatory spectrum, the second are more specific and the third deal with the particular issue of the codes of practice and guidelines used by regulatory authorities.

General principles of protection of privacy and the press

Any regulator should be committed to the following general principles:

- equality of access to privacy protection

  The aim of reform should be to guarantee equity of access to privacy protection, balanced only by a general presumption in favour of freedom of speech and social importance.

- proportionality: the use of a graded approach

  Codes and regulators should enable a scalable notion of privacy and the public interest and judge whether the degree of intrusion justifiable is proportionate to the 'social importance' of the story. For example, the illness of a famous musician may have a degree of social importance, but a low degree, and therefore would not justify say, using long lens photography.

- balancing certainty with flexibility

  The public, media professionals and regulators should have some certainty and clear expectations as to when they can assume that their privacy is protected. A lack of certainty is often as bad as no protection in terms of its chilling impact on journalistic practice and the freedom of public figures. Specific measures should be taken to inform journalists in detail of the implications of any regulatory reform so they are clear about their rights.

- responding to the challenge of media convergence and globalisation

  The regulator should develop new structures and principles of privacy protection that reflect not technologies so much as the degree of publicity and searchability they offer.

More specifically:

- injunctions granting prior restraint should only be used in the most serious of infringements and then only where there is no relevance to political, economic or democratic life.
- an appropriate penalty should be linked to severity of infringement and the amount of publicity the complainant has sought in the past.

Codes of practice

Many would argue that the problem is not with the content of the codes, but with their enforcement. There is a degree of truth in this, but nevertheless a clear code is essential for enforcement. We therefore suggest the following measures for the PCC code, the BSC and ITC codes (OFCOM), and the NUJ code of practice:

Regulators and the NUJ should:

- ensure HRA compliance by all codes and incorporation of Articles 8 and 10.
- specify regulations on all new surveillance technologies, not just long lens photography

- provide clarification of the term 'public interest', specifically mentioning that a significant level of public demand for a story is not sufficient justification for publication. Instead an editor should be able to show that (s)he had good reason to expect that the story would have an impact on the lives of many people.
- provide a stronger privacy clause for the NUJ code. Journalists and editors should be prepared to reaffirm quality news values and to demonstrate public interest before sanctioning intrusive news-gathering.

We also recommend that a review of HRA impact on journalism and privacy should be carried out by an independent commission should take place after a further two years, and that the Government should monitor the relationship between regulators and the courts.

Ensuring independent, effective regulation

The most important objective for any regulatory body is independence. Independence can be understood in different ways. A regulator might be a non-statutory body, independent from the government, or independent from the industry that it regulates, a feature common to statutory bodies but not necessarily confined to them.

The criticisms of statutory regulation of the media stem from the idea that it is unwise for the government to be able to influence reporting. The main criticism for self-regulation is that it the regulator will be too biased towards the industry that set it up and only act in the interests of consumers or citizens when it suits. As the communications market grows increasingly competitive, it is likely that self-regulation will become more common in the long term. It is necessary to begin thinking about the principles for strong, effective self-regulation while considering what a statutory body such as OFCOM will have to in the shorter term. The most important task for any regulator is to secure public confidence in the regulatory process. We suggest that if OFCOM or the PCC adopt the following principles, public confidence in both can be secured.

Maximum transparency

- Public and media and any other interested parties should have access to a complete explanation of what they can expect from a system, and the reasons and criteria for regulation
- Reports of cases should be made available to the public as soon as possible. If a case involves any form of prior restraint, then ideally the report should be available by the next day. A maximum time limit between the adjudication and the publishing of report should set.
- There should be an accessible and clear procedure for prior restraint, rather than the current ad hoc arrangements at the PCC which tend to protect only the privacy and reputation of a privileged few.

Emphasis should be placed on proactively ensuring that privacy violations do not occur. This could take several forms, such as:

- Commissioning research into the issue of privacy and media power, accepting third party complaints
- Instigating investigations rather than waiting for a public complaint
- Taking on a greater advisory role to the industry players, including issuing prior warnings that a publication might break the codes.

Lay and expert regulation

Effective regulation requires an appropriate balance of experts and lay people. We consider that there needs to be a greater lay participation in privacy regulation. We suggest that:

- each newspaper should appoint an ombudsman, who would be independent from the editor, and who would deal with complaints and issues and audit the standards of the paper. This initiative would also benefit other areas of regulation such as ownership issues.

- the number of lay members on the PCC adjudication panel should be increased.
- the current situation at the PCC which allows serving editors to be on the adjudication panel compromises the independence of the PCC. If expert views are sought, then former editors should be invited to the panel.

Sanctions

More effective sanctions, including the power to issue fines or award compensation, should be available and used. Self-regulatory bodies such as ICSTIS, the regulator of premium-rate telephony, do issue fines against their members, and such a move could serve to demonstrate the press's commitment to strong, effective self-regulation. An alternative could be to give the PCC power to refer persistent offenders to a statutory body, such as OFCOM, which will deal with broadcasting privacy issues, on the advertising regulation model. Giving a statutory body powers to fine or penalise should not be problematic. The ITC for example, can ultimately revoke a licence from a broadcaster. Publication of adjudications, or granting right of reply on the model of the BSC, is less appropriate as a sanction model for privacy breaches. If broadcasters are obliged to carry an adjudication they often are forced to do so in a particularly cryptic way, because it is the nature of privacy breaches that further publicity cannot satisfactorily reverse harm. More publicity may make matters worse.

A strategy for reform: a role for government?

We have shown that the Human Rights Act forces a rethink of how privacy issues are dealt with and outlined a series of sensible measures that can be taken to improve overall regulatory performance in this sensitive area. There is clearly some danger that this complex regulatory system will experience difficulties, which could result in worsening confusion for the industry. The Government should keep a watching brief on the regulation of journalistic intrusion as we adjust to the Human Rights Act. A sensible strategy in dealing with these issues is to see them as a sequence of approaches: if one fails, then recourse must be taken to the next.

- reform self-regulation

  History tells us that self-regulatory authorities improve dramatically in response to bad publicity or the threat of government regulation. The challenge for them is to improve performance without those spurs, and the competition threatened by use of the HRA in courts might encourage them to do so.

- accredit self-regulation

  Self-regulatory authorities could be independently assessed within clearly determined parameters, for example in relation to the enforcement of their code.

- allow case law to develop

  An independent review should be conducted in two years.

- introduce a privacy law

  In the event that the combination of an improved PCC, a new OFCOM code for the competitive electronic communications sector, and the HRA do not deliver adequate protection, a specific privacy law should be introduced. Government should make a clear announcement that it is not currently planning this, but will do so if necessary within the next Parliament.

If no action is taken with regard to privacy codes and their enforcement, it is likely that more high-profile privacy cases will be brought to court, and case law will develop slowly, based on cases brought by privacy entrepreneurs. A two-tier system of privacy regulation will develop; with those having the means to go to courts using the legal system, and everyone else complaining to a statutory or self-regulatory body. This will do nothing to combat the current inequalities in privacy violation or protection.

Introducing a privacy law

Legislating to introduce a law of privacy would remove many of the ambiguities and confusions in current privacy protection, and would have the advantage that the law would be made by elected representatives, not unelected judges. However such a move would be hugely controversial, and great care would be needed to ensure that such a law protects those who need it, and not those who would abuse it. In a democracy, it is still better to err on the side of freedom of information and expression wherever possible. If legislation is brought in, policy-makers would have to address the problem of ensuring that everyone has access to the law: as mentioned before, bringing a case to court is beyond the means of most people.

Legislation should be brought in only as a last resort, if the proposed changes to the current regulatory systems are shown to have failed. Although there are some legitimate doubts about the willingness of some sections of the media to reform their regulatory systems, the disadvantages of leaving case law to develop should provide a strong incentive. If privacy legislation is ever considered by parliament, the Government should be sensitive to the fact that such a law could be used in attempts to suppress legitimate reporting and must legislate accordingly. It will also be necessary to ensure that the high costs of legal procedures do not prevent the general public accessing justice.

Accordingly we recommend the following in the event that specific privacy legislation is considered:

- Any privacy bill must be balanced by a law to guarantee freedom of expression
- A tribunal system should be used to enforce privacy laws. This is cheaper and more informal than the court, and therefore more accessible

Conclusion

For the moment at least, we believe that the best option is to reform the current regulatory system so that it provides a credible alternative to the courts for everyone. Action is needed now to avoid the development of a two-tier regulatory system. As with any regulatory decision, the aims of any reform should be made absolutely clear from the start, and this is a job for Government. The operational aims of speed, flexibility, reduced cost and certainty, as well as accountability and proportionality, target-orientedness, transparency, and consistency (the objectives of the

Better Regulation Task Force) should be observed. The aim should be to create a system that is compliant with the Human Rights Act and which is strong and independent enough to regain the confidence of the public.

Endnotes

1. It is noteworthy that the Court of Appeal, in the case of *A v B and C*, set out guidelines to be observed by judges in determining applications for interim injunctions. These appear to be open to the criticism that they offer too imprecise a notion of the public interest. 'Even trivial facts relating to a public figure can be of great interest to readers and other observers of the media... The public figure may be a role model whose conduct could well be emulated by others... The courts must not ignore the fact that if newspapers do not publish information the public are interested in, there will be fewer newspapers published, which will not be in the public interest. The same is true in relation to other parts of the media'. (*A v B and C* [2002])
2. The extent to which the NUJ can be considered a branch of professional self-regulation in this respect is limited. The Union does not receive many complaints, and there is no record available of journalists being expelled from the Union for breach of the code.

References

A v B and C [2002] Jack J All ER 449 and CA EWCA Civ 337

Neill B (1999) 'Privacy: A challenge for the next century' in Markensis B (ed) *Protecting Privacy* Oxford University Press

Tomlinson H (ed) (2002) *Privacy and the Media: The developing law* Matrix Chambers Ltd

Weintraub J and Kumar K (eds) (1997) *Public and Private in Thought and Practice: perspectives on a grand dichotomy* University of Chicago Press

Warren and Brandeis (1890) 'The Right to Privacy' *Harvard Law Review* 193